Reclaiming
Prophetic Witness

Reclaiming Prophetic Witness

LIBERAL RELIGION IN THE PUBLIC SQUARE

Paul Rasor

Skinner House Books
BOSTON

www.skinnerhouse.org

Printed in the United States

Cover design by Bruce Jones
Text design by Jeff Miller

print ISBN: 978-1-55896-676-5
eBook ISBN: 978-1-55896-677-2

6 5 4 3
15 14

Library of Congress Cataloging-in-Publication Data

Rasor, Paul B.
  Reclaiming prophetic witness : liberal religion in the public square / Paul Rasor.
    p. cm.
  Includes bibliographical references.
  ISBN 978-1-55896-676-5 (pbk. : alk. paper) — ISBN 978-1-55896-677-2 (ebook)
  1. Religion and politics.   2. Liberalism (Religion)   I. Title.
  BL65.P7R37 2012
  261.70973 — dc23
                                                           2012010429

Contents

Foreword

THIS IS A TIME for prophets. In the United States, economic inequality—at its highest level since the Gilded Age—is tearing our communities apart, depriving young people of hope in the future. Across the world, the unsustainable use of fossil fuels has poisoned the soil and the air, turning African farms into desert and threatening island nations with destruction. Great liberation struggles of past generations remain incomplete. All too often, churches close their doors to queer families, schools close their doors to immigrant children, and hospitals close their doors to the most vulnerable. The earth and her people cry out in anguish, in indignation, and, yet still, in hope.

In times like these, prophets must speak loudly, clearly, and with many voices. We need prophets of economics to explain the cascading consequences of inequality and envision workplace democracy and socially responsible investment. We need prophets of science who can track the steady increase in global temperatures, chart its implications, and convey the urgency of those implications to policymakers. We need prophets of the arts to express their vision for social renewal in stirring songs and inspiring stories. We need prophets who testify to the human costs of inequality and oppression, and tell their stories of how individuals and communities are fighting back. And, of course, we need prophets of faith to bring the rich resources of religion into the struggle, making ancient traditions new by applying them to today's challenges. In times like these, religion can provide us with words of judgment, speaking truth to power: "What do you mean by crushing my people, and grinding down the poor?" (Isaiah 3:15) It can offer us words of mourning, when our "eyes flow without ceasing . . . Till the Lord from heaven looks down and sees" (Lamentations 3:49–50). And it can offer words of hope, promising a just future in which people "shall beat their swords into plowshares" (Micah 4:3) and "the mountains shall drip new wine, and the hills shall flow with milk" (Joel 4:18).

We need prophets with hands strong enough to smash the golden calves of plutocracy, hearts big enough to declare "jubilee" to all who are burdened with debts they can never repay, and voices loud enough to be heard in the halls of Congress and the boardrooms of business. And yet, it is not easy to find one's prophetic voice. When Moses encountered the divine in the burning bush, he protested that he was "slow of speech and tongue," unable to command the attention of the Israelites (Exodus 4:10). Frederick Douglass, the great abolitionist orator, described his first speech to a white audience as a "severe cross" because he "still felt myself a slave."

We who are called to prophetic witness today face our own set of obstacles. Religious liberals, in particular, have so often been offended and appalled by the prophets of conservative Christianity that we silence ourselves rather than risk sounding like them. Because we cherish the American experiment in religious freedom, we may worry that public witness in the name of faith could violate the separation of church and state. Our respect for the personal convictions of others may cause us to recoil from the harsh and denunciatory language favored by the biblical prophets. Drawing on a long tradition of openness to culture, we may find it hard to adopt the critical stance of the prophets, even as we see glaring injustices right in front of us.

This book is a handbook for prophets like us. Speaking directly to religious liberals, Paul Rasor lays out our shortcomings in sometimes painful detail. Too often, we cede the public square to religious conservatives. Too often, we speak out in neutral language that does not convey our deepest values and hopes. We imagine that we are too few to make a difference, failing to see that liberal ideals are held by at least a fifth of the American population.

Rasor calls us to do better—and provides us with the tools for the task. Drawing on sources as varied as political philosophy, demographic surveys, and biblical studies, he shows that it is possible for religious liberals to speak out without compromising our convictions or our sensibilities. By urging us to reclaim prophetic witness, he calls us to strengthen our identity as religious liberals. When we know deeply that all of humanity—indeed, all life—is connected, and that each of us has inherent worth and dignity, we will not hesitate to challenge attacks on that dignity or the ways we are held together. And in so doing, we will help to heal the world.

—Dan McKanan

Introduction

In December 2011, Rick Perry, governor of Texas campaigning to become the Republican candidate in the 2012 presidential election, declared in a campaign commercial,

> I'm not ashamed to admit that I'm a Christian. But you don't need to be in the pew every Sunday to know there's something wrong in this country when gays can serve openly in the military but our kids can't openly celebrate Christmas or pray in school. As president, I'll end Obama's war on religion. And I'll fight against liberal attacks on our religious heritage. Faith made America strong. It can make her strong again. I'm Rick Perry and I approve this message.[1]

Meanwhile, on November 24, 2011, FOX News Radio host Todd Starnes criticized President Barack Obama for omitting any reference to God in his Thanksgiving Day proclamation. Starnes noted that the president's remarks "were void of any religious references, although Thanksgiving is a holiday traditionally steeped in giving thanks and praise to God."[2] FOX was not alone; several other media sources published similar criticisms.[3]

The Perry ad and the FOX News response typify the dominant form of public religious expression in the United States: theologically conservative, self-assured, and pervasive. From the perspective of religious liberalism, they are also deeply troubling. Perry's statement reflects one common pattern. Cloaked in the language of religious freedom, it in fact constitutes a serious threat to religious freedom and to civil liberties generally. Perry suggests that eligibility for service in the military, and by implication other forms of public service, including the presidency, should be determined by the values of one particular religious perspective — conservative Christianity. He also suggests that anyone with a different religious view is antireligious and unfit for office. In other words, he assumes that despite America's historical and constitutionally guaranteed tradition of religious pluralism, there is only one proper religious viewpoint, and that viewpoint should determine public policy.

The pervasiveness of these sorts of messages is also troubling; they are not simply a feature of Republican presidential politics. Major television and other news outlets support this theological perspective. One liberal watchdog organization calls FOX News "the mouthpiece for the evangelical religious right."[4] Conservative evangelicals promote their views on the national stage through media outlets such as the Christian Broadcasting Network (CBN), founded by television evangelist Pat Robertson in 1961 and broadcast worldwide; Trinity Broadcasting Network (TBN); and the Inspiration Network, originally founded as PTL Satellite Network by Jim and Tammy Faye Bakker, among others. Over the past few decades, the dominant religious voices in the United States have come from the religious right, and they have been important allies for conservative political and social agendas. Religious liberals, meanwhile, seem to have moved into the background of public life or disappeared altogether.[5] A casual observer of the religious scene in the United States today — the proverbial visitor from Mars, say — could be forgiven for thinking that religious liberalism is a movement whose time has passed.

Religious liberals themselves must accept much of the responsibility for this sad state of affairs. Several studies confirm what many of us have known implicitly for several years, namely that religiously grounded social justice work has declined among religious liberals. This situation is as ironic as it is unfortunate. Religious liberalism has always understood itself as a prophetic tradition oriented toward social justice. Yet these studies show that in recent years, religious liberals have been far less likely than members of other religious groups to support any form of activism or speaking out on public issues by their clergy or denominational leaders, and they have been less likely to engage in most forms of political participation.[6] A telling question in a 2004 survey asked whether religious groups should stand up for their beliefs. Less than two-thirds of religious liberals agreed that they should, the lowest percentage for any group. And only 15 percent of liberals said that religion was important to their political thinking, in contrast to 81 percent of conservative evangelicals and 39 percent of the population as a whole. These studies suggest that religious liberals are far more likely than other groups to separate their religious convictions from their political activities.[7]

The news media have contributed to this perception. While conservatives often complain of the media's liberal bias, its coverage of religion actually reflects a conservative bias. A 2007 study by Media Matters for America, a nonprofit media-monitoring organization, found that during the two-year period following the 2004 presidential elections, the major news media covered or quoted conservative religious figures nearly three times more often than progressive figures. This skewed media coverage is compounded by the widespread but erroneous assumption that religious convictions are not relevant to liberal activism. Religious liberals will not be covered if the media does not recognize their existence. Instead, conservative figures are overwhelmingly presented as the voice of religion in America, while liberal religious voices are ignored or marginalized.[8]

The American public seems to share the unfortunate assumption that political liberals can't be religious. Journalist and political commentator E. J. Dionne provides an interesting example of this stereotype from the 2005 Virginia gubernatorial election. Liberal Democratic candidate Tim Kaine, who won the election, often spoke publicly about the ways his religious values informed his political positions. Yet when focus groups were shown footage of Kaine making such comments, they were nearly unanimous in believing that "if Kaine was religious, he could not possibly be a liberal."[9] This bias both draws on and perpetuates the unfortunate stereotype that sees America divided by a culture war between the secular left and the religious right. The result is an overly simplistic worldview that equates liberal with secular and conservative with religious, and liberal religion becomes invisible.

There are several possible explanations for the relatively low involvement among religious liberals. In some cases, declining numbers plays a role. Congregations worried about survival tend to turn inward rather than outward and may avoid activities that could be seen as controversial.[10] Another factor is the emergence of the religious right as a major force in American life since the late 1970s, and the corresponding shift in media and scholarly attention away from religious liberalism. One observer suggests that liberals have grown complacent, perhaps as a result of their own earlier accomplishments in areas such as civil rights, nuclear disarmament, and environmental protection.[11] Theological factors are also at work here. Religious liberals tend to avoid using specifically religious language in their public activities, perhaps out of fear that the media will ignore or distort their message, and this can lead them to disguise their religious commitments. Moreover, mistrust of religious dogma and openness to diverse theological traditions, while generally a positive trait, can leave religious liberals uncertain about how to relate their faith commitments to their social and political commitments.

The news is not all bad. The fact that religious liberals have been less visible does not mean that they have stopped their prophetic social justice practice altogether. Liberal and mainline churches have long been involved in education, community organizations, and various forms of volunteer work, and this work has continued.[12] A 2009 study on religious activism notes that progressive religious activists have become somewhat more visible during the past few years.[13] One example is Unitarian Universalists, whom political scientist John Green calls "the quintessential liberal denomination in the United States." Green notes that Unitarian Universalist clergy have remained a highly activist "dynamo of the left in contemporary American politics" by translating their theology into social and political activism.[14] Unitarian Universalist activism shows no signs of slowing down; if anything, it has accelerated at the levels of both reflection and action. In 2008, the Unitarian Universalist Association (UUA) launched its Standing on the Side of Love campaign in response to the shooting at the Tennessee Valley Unitarian Universalist Church in Knoxville. This campaign has expanded into a vehicle for focusing attention on a range of justice issues.[15] In July 2010, for example, approximately 150 Unitarian Universalists from around the country—all wearing bright yellow T-shirts emblazoned with the Standing on the Side of Love logo—participated in a highly publicized protest against Arizona's harsh and unjust immigration laws. Rev. Peter Morales, UUA president, and Rev. Susan Frederick Gray, minister of the Unitarian Universalist Congregation of Phoenix, were among those arrested during the demonstrations and later convicted of misdemeanor charges.[16] The UUA followed up these events by joining other activist groups to create an advocacy toolkit that provides resources to those working for more humane immigration policies.[17] As this book went to press, the 2012 Unitarian Universalist General Assembly was about to meet in Phoenix to focus specifically on issues of social justice.

Religious liberals have long been active in promoting same-sex marriage and other equal rights for gay, lesbian, bisexual, and transgender people. The Standing on the Side of Love campaign has identified this as a special project, and the United Church of Christ (UCC) became the first mainline Protestant church to support same-sex marriage in 2005.[18] This followed the UCC's God is Still Speaking campaign, whose message, "No matter who you are, or where you are on life's journey, you're welcome here," was designed in part to reach out to gay and lesbian people looking for a church home.[19]

Despite these and other examples of liberal religious involvement in work for political and social change at the institutional level, the sad truth is that individual religious liberals are far less likely than other groups to see social justice activism as religious work. Religious liberals on the whole tend to hold religious beliefs with less conviction than their conservative counterparts, and this affects their ability to carry their beliefs into practice. Charles F. Andrain, an astute observer of the relationship between religion and justice in the United States, concludes that "the prospect for liberal churches securing fundamental [social] transformations appears limited."[20]

It is both ironic and tragic that we have come full circle since the civil rights era of the 1950s and 1960s, when no one doubted that religion was an important force for progressive social change, and religious liberals were among the movement's leading voices. Indeed, religious liberals have been influential advocates for social reform at least since the abolition and suffrage movements of the early nineteenth century. As political scientist Alan Wolfe points out, "If people engaged in political debate today went back to their roots, we would likely have a secular right in the United States being confronted by a religious left."[21] Instead, the opposite seems to be the case. The near-disappearance of religious liberals from American public life places this long tradition of liberal religious activism at risk.

This book explores a series of dilemmas that affects liberal religious social justice work, or what I call *liberal prophetic practice* or *prophetic liberalism*. These dilemmas include theological tensions inherent in religious liberalism that sometimes cause us to stumble over our best intentions; the impact of the ongoing debate about the proper role of religion in the public square; confusion about what it means to speak religiously; the tension that emerges from religious liberals' commitment to separation of church and state; and the challenge of engaging in public prophetic practice under conditions of empire. The book concludes with some reflections on religious identity, a critically important yet perennially difficult issue for religious liberals.

My primary focus throughout this book is liberal religion in the United States, and while I hope to speak to a broad range of religious liberals, my analysis will no doubt reflect my own Unitarian Universalist perspective. However, as chapter one makes clear, religious liberalism encompasses far more than a single denomination or religious tradition. Issues concerning the proper relationship between religion and politics, and the role and effectiveness of the liberal prophetic voice, are widely discussed by religious liberals around the globe. While I have participated in and benefitted from many of these ongoing discussions, I cannot directly address these wider international concerns here. Nevertheless, I hope that what I offer here will contribute something useful to religious liberals facing these issues elsewhere.

Religious Liberalism, Alive and Well

THIS BOOK AIMS, in part, to help reverse the lamentable public retreat of religious liberals in recent decades. Yet, religious liberalism on the whole in the United States is by no means diminishing. Recent studies indicate that approximately one in four Americans describe themselves as religious liberals, roughly the same number as those who describe themselves as religious conservatives—and some suggest that the number of religious liberals may be even higher. To make sense of the numbers, we need to define *religious liberal.*

While there are many ways to describe religious liberalism, scholars generally agree that its most prominent characteristic is a posture of intentional engagement with modern culture.[22] Religious liberalism starts with the premise that religion should be oriented toward the present, not the past, and that religious beliefs should be in tune with modern knowledge and experience.

This adaptive orientation can be traced to liberalism's roots in the Enlightenment. Rather than resist the Enlightenment's modernizing ideas, as religious orthodoxies tried to do, liberals embraced them. As a result, religious ideas are often stated in terms of the language and values of contemporary culture. Liberal beliefs about God or the nature of the universe, for example,

1

typically take into account the perspectives of modern science. In the late nineteenth century, liberal theologians were the first to incorporate the theory of evolution into their work,[23] and they continue to draw on evolutionary biology and other features of modern scientific thought. By the same token, religious liberals' assessments of social issues normally draw more on the findings and methodologies of the social sciences than on explanations rooted in scripture or tradition. As a result, liberals are not likely to feel their faith threatened by new scientific discoveries or advances in biblical scholarship. Instead, they accept these kinds of developments and incorporate them into their religious world-views. In this way, liberals seek to keep their religious commitments culturally relevant and intellectually credible. Theologian Sallie McFague says that

> we should aim for coherence or compatibility between the scientific view and the interpretation of our basic doctrine. . . . [A] theology that avoids this task and settles for an outmoded view is irresponsible and will eventually be seen to be incredible.[24]

A second characteristic of religious liberalism is a commitment to free religious inquiry. This commitment encourages religious liberals to exercise their own independent judgment in matters of faith. For liberals, religious authority is based on individual reason and experience rather than external sources such as scripture or the church. This means that no truth claim can be accepted simply because it is steeped in tradition or because the church or some other established authority declares it to be so. Liberals place far less emphasis on matters of doctrine than their conservative counterparts, and give priority instead to matters of social ethics. They are comfortable with the notion that religious doctrines change over time, that experience can be reinterpreted, and that today's best ideas may be rejected as absurd tomorrow. Liberal theologians are likely to say that religious meaning is constructed rather than given,[25] and to reject the idea that truth is given just once for all time. In a typically liberal move, theologian James Luther Adams insisted that because reality is continuously recreated, no belief system or historical moment may claim special status.[26] As a result, religious liberals tend to have open-ended and flexible faith commitments and to be comfortable with religious pluralism.

Beyond these general characteristics, surveys of American religious identity typically use a set of more specific criteria. Political scientist John Green, director of the Bliss Institute of Applied Politics at the University of Akron, has developed a methodology that measures patterns of religious belief and behavior for a range of specific factors and then uses the results to identify three basic categories of people: traditionalists, centrists, and modernists.[27] We may think of them as conservative, moderate, and liberal. Factors measured in this approach include beliefs about God, an afterlife, the Bible, the devil, evolution, and the truth of other religions, as well as certain patterns of religious behavior and levels of religious engagement. For example, religious liberals are more likely than religious conservatives to think of God as a type of impersonal force or universal spirit rather than an anthropomorphic being. Similarly, religious liberals typically view scripture as the work of human writers in particular historical circumstances rather than the word of God, and to see religions other than their own as also containing religious truth or as leading to some form of salvation.

Historically, discussions of American religion commonly—and understandably—refer to liberalism as a category within Christianity, often within Protestant Christianity. Liberalism originated largely as a challenge to Calvinist orthodoxies among Universalists and Unitarians in the late eighteenth and early nineteenth centuries, and spread to other Protestant traditions in the second half of the nineteenth century.[28] A liberal movement within American Roman Catholicism emerged around the turn of the twentieth century but was squelched by Vatican authorities, and not until the 1960s did liberal Catholicism become well established.[29] Interestingly, recent polls indicate that American Catholics today are on the whole more religiously liberal than American Protestants.[30]

Many people are unaware that religious liberalism in the United States reaches well beyond Christianity. We commonly describe fundamentalism as a strand that runs through nearly every religious group, even though the term originally applied to a specific movement within Christianity. The same can be said of liberalism. All religious groups in the United States include significant numbers of liberals; indeed, most have a higher percentage of religious liberals than Christianity.

Reform Judaism is perhaps the most familiar example. Like liberal Protestantism, Reform Judaism emerged in the wake of the Enlightenment, and one of its central commitments is the importance of adapting to modern culture. The Reform platform adopted in the United States in 1885 declares, in part:

> We hold that the modern discoveries of scientific researches in the domain of nature and history are not antagonistic to the doctrines of Judaism, the Bible reflecting the primitive ideas of its own age. . . . [We] reject all [moral laws] as are not adapted to the views and habits of modern civilization. . . . We recognize in Judaism a progressive religion, ever striving to be in accord with the postulates of reason.[31]

In the United States today, four in ten Jews (41 percent) belong to Reform Judaism, by far the largest group within American Judaism.[32]

Jewish liberalism extends beyond the Reform movement. Conservative Judaism, despite its name, is also largely religiously liberal. Like Reform Judaism, Conservative Judaism accepts the need to adapt to modern culture, although it also seeks to preserve the knowledge and practices of historical tradition. The number of Jews affiliated with Conservative congregations in the United States has declined in recent years, now constituting just under 30 percent of the American Jewish population.[33] Together, Reform and Conservative Judaism account for 70 percent of this population. Therefore, most American Jews are religious liberals.[34] Indeed, according to typical survey measures, Jews on the whole register far more liberal than nearly all other groups.[35]

Muslims also count many religious liberals among their number, although for the most part, American Muslims are religiously mainstream. While Muslims tend to hold orthodox beliefs on traditional tenets, such as belief in a Day of Judgment, a majority hold more liberal views regarding the interpretation of Muslim teachings, the non-exclusivity of the Muslim path to salvation, and attitudes toward modern society. Overall, in recent surveys, Muslim responses on these topics were similar to those of mainline Protestants.[36] Various forms of liberalism may also be found among American Buddhists, Hindus, and persons of other religious traditions. Indeed, the survey data indicates that overall, Christians are the least religiously liberal of all groups. Viewing it from this broad perspective, and not simply as a movement within Christianity, will provide a better understanding of religious liberalism in the United States.

Religious Liberals and Religious Pluralism

It has been said, although not quite accurately, that the United States is "the world's most religiously diverse nation."[37] To get a true picture of religious liberalism, therefore, we need to locate it within the context of this vast pluralism.

Pluralism of all kinds is an inevitable feature of any democracy that values freedom of speech and association. When church and state are formally separated, as in the United States, religious pluralism will be especially pronounced. American religious pluralism is unique not only because of its astonishing breadth, but because it was encouraged by the nation's founders. In other Western democracies, religious diversity has most often appeared when previously established religious unity collapsed. By contrast, the founders of the United States presupposed and accepted pluralism as the best means of protecting both religious and political liberty. James Madison, for example, famously insisted that a "multiplicity of sects . . . is the best and only security for religious liberty in any society. For where there is such a variety of sects, there cannot be a majority of any one sect to oppress and persecute the rest."[38]

Of course, the pluralism Madison envisioned consisted mainly within a range of Christian denominations, although even then America's religious diversity was broader than most of the founders were prepared to acknowledge. In addition to the diverse native cultures throughout the land, Jews were present in large numbers in several mid-Atlantic regions,[39] and enslaved people often practiced the Islamic or African traditions they had brought to America.[40] These religious traditions remain part of the American landscape today. But Christianity was the common reference point for the European colonists, and public discourse could still assume a set of common religious and moral reference points.

The American religious landscape is far more complex today. The diversity both within and among religious groups vastly exceeds anything Madison and the other founders could have envisioned. Not only is Christianity shrinking as a percentage of the population, but the radical diversity *within* Christianity means that the term no longer (if it ever did) identifies a cohesive theological or cultural group. Over time, Christianity's theological spectrum gradually extended at both ends. The decades around the turn of the twentieth century—scarcely a century after Madison's call for multiplicity—witnessed simultaneously the prominence of Protestant theological liberalism, the social gospel movement, the appearance of Christian fundamentalism, a huge increase in the numbers and diversity of American Jews and Roman Catholics, and the emergence of new religious movements such as Pentecostalism and Christian Science.[41] This process has continued throughout the twentieth century and into the twenty-first. Today, as for most of the preceding century, the term *Christian* is claimed by individuals and groups whose theological orientations are fundamentally incompatible.

Christians, although still a significant majority, represent a rapidly decreasing percentage of the U.S. population, dropping from 86 to 76 percent in less than two decades.[42] Protestants, for a century and a half the de facto established faith, but barely a majority today at 51 percent, will surely soon drop below 50 percent. The Pew Religious Landscape survey finds that "the United States is on the verge of becoming a minority Protestant country."[43] Moreover, the liberal-conservative-fundamentalist divide within Christianity—indeed, within many single denominations—suggests that it may no longer be meaningful to speak of a Protestant or even a Christian majority. In a sense, we are all religious minorities now.

Diversity within Christianity is only the beginning. Changes to U.S. immigration policy in the 1960s brought to our shores millions of people from around the world practicing Muslim, Hindu, Buddhist, Sikh, Afro-Caribbean, and other faiths. While their numbers are still relatively small — these traditions together make up about 4 percent of the U.S. population — many of them are among the fastest-growing faiths. Both their increasing numbers and their increased visibility have made Americans of all faiths more aware than in previous generations of the diverse religious reality to which we all belong. This is the larger context within which religious liberalism, as a multi-faith reality, must come to understand itself.

Religious Liberals and the Religious Left

Over the past decade, there has been much discussion about the reemergence of the religious left as a force in American public and political life.[44] This development and the attention it is receiving are welcome news. However, precisely because of this renewed attention, we must be careful not to confuse the *religious left* with *religious liberalism*. The two terms are not interchangeable.

Religious left is as much a political as a religious term. It is most often used to describe persons who support liberal-progressive social and political positions as a result of their religious convictions. However, these religious convictions need not be liberal in the sense described above. As First Amendment scholar Steven Shiffrin notes, the term *religious left* refers to those who "arrive at liberal political conclusions in accordance with religious premises whether those premises are thought to be theologically

8

liberal or more traditional."[45] While many, perhaps most, religious liberals might share the same progressive social and political positions, those on the religious left represent a broad range of theological orientations. Examples include activist Jim Wallis, leader of the Sojourners community, whose commitment to social justice is evangelical and scripture-based,[46] and Rabbi Michael Lerner, editor of *Tikkun* magazine, a publication that brings together agnostic and religious social progressives from many faith traditions.[47] One recent study concludes that religious liberals constitute only 52 percent of progressive religious activists, while 10 percent identify as evangelical Protestants.[48]

Counting Liberals

The misperception that religious liberalism is not prevalent in the United States may be partly due to the common tendency to link being religious with being conservative. The dominance of conservative religious voices in public discussion surely feeds this perception. Yet there are at least as many religious liberals as religious conservatives in the United States today. This makes liberals' relative invisibility all the more surprising.

Counting religious liberals is not a simple task. First, the available data comes primarily from surveys of American religious identity that rarely use the term *liberal* as a reporting category. Christians are typically identified in terms of three major groups — evangelical Protestant, mainline Protestant, and Roman Catholic — as well as a number of smaller categories that may be general ("other Christian," "Christian unspecified") or specific (Mormon, Jehovah's Witness, Orthodox). Most surveys include separate categories for Jews and Muslims, but many lump others together as "Eastern Religions" or "other non-Christian." The "other" category may also include a range of diverse smaller groups, such as Unitarian Universalist, New Age, or Native American.[49]

Second, individuals in these groups are not uniform. While it is true that mainline Protestants are on the whole more theologically liberal than evangelical Protestants, one cannot determine the number of religious liberals, or even liberal Protestants, simply by counting the mainline population. Whatever reporting categories are used in the surveys, all groups include individuals from across the theological spectrum. This means that religious liberals may be found in many—probably most—of these groups. Moreover, religious liberals themselves are not all alike. Individuals are more or less liberal, even within the definitional reference points examined earlier. There is no simple way to count the number of religious liberals.

Despite these difficulties, however, the surveys do provide a wealth of data from which we can reach a useful estimate. Using the methodology described above, the 2004 and 2008 Bliss Institute surveys divide each of the three largest Christian groups—evangelical Protestant, mainline Protestant, and Catholic—into three subcategories: traditionalist, centrist, and modernist. Thus, in addition to reporting the relevant percentages of evangelical and mainline Protestants, for example, these surveys give us data for traditionalist evangelicals and traditionalist mainliners, centrist evangelicals and centrist mainliners, and modernist evangelicals and modernist mainliners. The same breakdown is given for non-Latino Roman Catholics. We can therefore calculate a reasonable baseline number for religious liberals simply by totaling the number of modernists in these three groups.

In the 2008 survey, the modernists represent 18.2% of the U.S. adult population, approximately the same as the total percentage of traditionalists, 18.6%. But this is only the starting point. We know religious liberals will be found in the other survey categories as well. One of these turns out to be easy—a category identified simply as "liberal faiths," representing 1.3% of the population.[50] This brings the number of religious liberals to 19.5%, or one-fifth, of the U.S. population.

Yet the number of religious liberals is almost certainly higher. The traditionalist/centrist/modernist breakdown was applied only to three main Christian groups. While they are the largest groups, together they represent less than 60% of the U.S. population. As noted earlier, adherents of other faiths are on the whole more religiously liberal than Christians, so if we include the number of liberal Jews, Buddhists, and others, the total percentages will increase a bit, perhaps to 21% or 22%.[51]

Another important study containing specific data about religious liberals is the Princeton Religion and Politics Survey published in 2000.[52] The Princeton survey used two techniques that are especially helpful for our inquiry. First, in addition to identifying respondents according to the usual denominational and faith categories, it also asked all respondents—not only Christians—to dentify themselves within a range of general religious perspectives. Catholics were given three choices: traditional, moderate, or liberal; all other Christians and non-Christians had four options: fundamentalist, evangelical, mainline, or liberal. The results of this inquiry are striking. Among Christians, 21.4% of Protestants and other non-Catholics identified themselves as religiously liberal, while 28.8% of Catholics identified as liberal. These groups constitute three-quarters of the U.S. population, with Protestants and "other" Christians representing two-thirds of this total. Interpolating the numbers indicates that approximately 24% of all Christians self-identify as religiously liberal, a figure nearly identical to those who identify as conservative.[53]

When non-Christians are factored in, the number of religious liberals is even higher. Significantly, nearly 30% of the respondents in the "other Religion (not Christian)" and "no preference" groups self-identified as liberal.[54] These groups constitute 18.7% of the overall population. When we factor them into the total for Christians, we see that more than one-quarter (26.2%) of adult Americans see themselves as religious liberals.

The second technique used by the Princeton survey is even more telling. All respondents — again, not only Christians — were asked to locate their own religious views along a 6-point scale ranging from "very conservative" (1) to "very liberal" (6). While a large plurality identified as moderate (43% chose either 3 or 4 on the 6-point scale), significantly more identified as liberal than as conservative: 30.2% chose either 5 or 6, the liberal end of the scale, while only 22.3% chose either 1 or 2, the conservative end. And 17.2% of respondents chose "very liberal" to describe their religious views, compared with only 12.4% who chose "very conservative." Of course, survey results based on self-identification are subjective; what is religiously liberal or moderate to one person may be conservative to another. Yet these risks seem likely to even out. And even allowing for this ambiguity, the results are striking. They would likely come as a surprise to those who think that religious liberalism has withered in the face of an aggressive religious right.

These overall findings are consistent with the widely cited 2008 Pew Religious Landscape Survey on American religious beliefs and practices.[55] Because it did not ask respondents to identify themselves on a liberal-conservative scale, nor report its results in terms of the traditionalist/centrist/modernist categories used in the Bliss surveys, we cannot use it to glean any specific data on religious liberals. However, the Pew survey did include findings on patterns of religious belief and behavior that are largely comparable to those used in the Bliss surveys, and these do permit some useful observations.

For example, the Pew survey shows that while Americans overwhelmingly (92%) claim to believe in God, only 60% believe that God is a person or being with whom they can have a personal relationship, while 25% hold the more liberal belief that God is a form of impersonal force or universal spirit. Similarly, 63% of Americans believe their sacred text is the word of God rather than simply the words of human beings, while 28% hold the more liberal view that their sacred text was written by human beings and should not be understood as the word of God. These percentages are consistent with the Princeton results.

On the whole, Americans are more liberal when it comes to attitudes toward other religions. The Pew survey indicates that 70% of Americans who have a religious affiliation believe that many religions can lead to salvation, while only 24% hold the exclusivist view that their religion is the only true path. Significantly, this pattern is present even in the more theologically conservative traditions. Only 36% of evangelical Protestants believe their religion is the one true faith, approximately the same percentage as Muslims (33%).

Finally, the Pew survey includes findings on attitudes toward modernity. Here too the results indicate broad acceptance of liberal ideas. Among Americans who have a religious affiliation, 54% see no conflict between being devout and living in modern society, although a substantial minority, 40%, do see such a conflict. Similarly, nearly half (47%) say that their religious tradition should adjust to new circumstances or adopt modern beliefs and practices, while 44% hold the traditionalist view that their religion should preserve its traditional beliefs and practices. These findings are consistent across nearly all religious traditions.

While this informal review of the Pew findings cannot be translated into precise percentages of religious conservatives, moderates, and liberals, it nevertheless confirms the basic results of the Bliss and Princeton surveys. In the end, we can say that at least a quarter of adult Americans, and perhaps as many as three in ten, may fairly be described as religious liberals—a reality about which the media and the American public remain sadly ignorant.

Prophetic Tensions in
Liberal Religion

F<small>ROM ITS</small> <small>BEGINNINGS</small>, American religious liberalism has included a prophetic dimension oriented toward social justice. This prophetic impulse is rooted in the tradition of the biblical prophets, who called society and its leaders to account for injustice, especially on behalf of its poorest and most marginalized members. Religious liberals affirm a vision of a more just society and a religious obligation to speak out against, and work to overcome, conditions that interfere with fulfilling this vision. Unitarian Universalist theologian James Luther Adams claimed that this religious imperative "makes the role of the prophet central and indispensable in liberalism."[56] Our history gives us countless examples of this practice, such as Theodore Parker, Frederick Douglass and Harriet Beecher Stowe in the nineteenth century, Walter Rauschenbusch, John Haynes Holmes and Jane Addams in the early twentieth century, and William Sloane Coffin and Martin Luther King Jr., among many others, in the mid-twentieth century. This heritage forms an important part of our liberal religious identity.

Paradoxically, many of the deepest commitments held by religious liberals seem to encourage traits that can undermine those very commitments. For example, a critical element of prophetic practice is religiously grounded critique of social injustice. But while contemporary religious liberals are not shy about speaking out on important social and political issues, they are often reluctant to do so using specifically religious language. This suspicion of religious language is one of several tensions within liberal religion that pull against liberalism's prophetic impulse. We need to understand these tensions if we want to reclaim a strong prophetic voice. If we cannot entirely eliminate them—they are, after all, inherent in the liberal tradition—we should be able to recognize when they are holding us back and make the necessary corrections.

Cultural Engagement

Most of the counter-prophetic tendencies in religious liberalism can be linked to its largely positive orientation toward modern culture. This perspective does more than encourage liberals to interpret religious texts in light of historical scholarship and keep their theologies consistent with modern science. It also encourages them to become actively engaged with the world—to embrace the world, not withdraw from it; to live fully *in* the world while bringing their religious values to bear *on* it. Liberal theologian Peter Hodgson argues that this engagement is essential if liberals are to fulfill their vision of a just society: "without actual engagement in the messy realities of the world, cultural transformation is not a possibility."[57]

But prophetic practice requires both cultural engagement and theological distance. It must be grounded in religious values independent of cultural norms so that it has clear reference points for forming judgments. At the same time, its theological reference points cannot be so foreign that its critique becomes incomprehensible. The prophet thus lives in this tension between participation and independence, standing both inside and outside society.

The biblical prophets did not have to deal with such tensions. One of their most important roles was to help preserve the proper covenantal relationship between God and the people. The prophets were understood as speaking directly for God, and they stood beyond the authority of the political leaders. Their critiques were grounded in the values of the covenant by which all social, political, and religious aspects of early Israel's communal life were ordered.[58] When Amos condemns the leaders and merchants of Israel as "you that trample on the needy, and bring ruin to the poor of the land,"[59] there is no doubt whose message he is delivering and whose norms they are being judged by.

In contemporary American society, with its formal separation of church and state and its radical religious and moral pluralism, the prophetic task is more complicated. Our political leaders are structurally independent of any particular religious perspective. Some conservative religious leaders and political candidates seem to believe that only evangelical Christians are qualified to lead the nation, but the American founders created a constitutional system that makes religion officially irrelevant when assessing the worth of someone's positions on public issues or qualifications to hold public office.[60] This important part of our constitutional system prevents any religious group's particular beliefs from becoming the basis for law or public policy, just as no political authority can dictate the doctrines of religious groups. This structure would seem to make it difficult for religiously grounded prophetic voices to be understood by those in the political sphere.

Yet many of our most basic understandings of legal justice have deep religious—often biblical—roots, and religiously based moral values permeate modern culture. Moreover, religion and politics in the United States have never been completely separated. Most political leaders claim to be religious, usually Christian, and many flaunt their religion as a way of identifying with a particular group of voters. Recent years have witnessed the sad and troubling spectacle of political candidates trying to out-Christian each other, often challenging other candidates' religious bona fides. Some voters' worries about 2012 Republican presidential candidate Mitt Romney's Mormonism echo the fearmongering of those who spread the bogus rumors that President Barack Obama is Muslim. (The question no one seems to ask is, So what?) These developments are troubling. From the perspective of prophetic practice, however, religiously grounded criticism of these political practices, or of governmental policies harmful to immigrants or the poor, for example, is not foreign to political leaders.

Many of the values dear to religious liberals, such as freedom, equality, and respect for each individual's dignity and worth, are also among the values that underlie democratic political structures. They persist even when particular political programs or economic practices undermine them. Indeed, the failure to honor these basic values invites prophetic critique. The greatest twentieth-century prophets, such as civil rights leader Martin Luther King Jr., often employed both religious and political language when speaking out for social justice. In fact, King's appeal to democratic values was deeply grounded in the biblical prophets' practice of seeking justice for the poor and marginalized. The Hebrew prophets in turn grounded their messages in the shared values of the covenant—but they also drew on cultural sources, including law courts, military practice, and political custom.[61]

Because of its orientation toward cultural engagement, religious liberalism is ideally situated to hold creatively the prophetic tension between independence and participation. In practice, however, this orientation can easily interfere with the liberal prophetic impulse. We can better understand how this can happen if we look at a common practice among religious conservatives. Religious liberals often criticize religious conservatives for being too closely identified with political conservatives, especially with the extreme right wing of the Republican Party. Liberals are correct to worry that this association would create a serious threat to religious freedom if this group increases its political power. From the perspective of prophetic practice, however, this close identification creates a different problem. It makes religiously based critique of their political allies extremely difficult—though many religious conservatives are not bashful about criticizing those who stray too far from the accepted dogma on abortion, same sex marriage, and other issues.

Religious liberals face a similar risk to their prophetic practice. This risk stems from religious liberalism's easy accommodation to modern culture rather than a desire for political power. The problem is that cultural adaptation—the very trait that defines us as religious liberals—can easily lead to comfortable familiarity, and comfort can weaken prophetic energy. Theologian H. Richard Niebuhr noted more than half a century ago that the liberal accommodation of religion and culture tends to produce a level of intellectual and social comfort, and that as a result, religious liberals tend to resist radical social change.[62] Philosopher and activist Cornel West argues that a strong prophetic voice requires resisting religious accommodation to the cultural status quo.[63]

Another dimension of liberalism's posture of engagement is its tendency to blur the distinction between religion and culture. This blurring is largely intentional. Religious liberals regard any separation of religion and culture as artificial and refuse to create moral distinctions between them. While this approach supports the social engagement required for prophetic practice, it also points to an important problem. Critics contend that liberalism's cultural orientation amounts to a total capitulation to culture. This criticism is misguided; religious liberalism's core theological commitments do support a clear prophetic stance. But the liberal refusal to draw a sharp line between religion and culture can make it difficult to maintain the necessary theological clarity needed to ground an effective prophetic voice. Religious identity may become so thin that liberal religion becomes indistinguishable from liberal politics, liberal spirituality dissolves into pop psychology, and liberalism's prophetic edge becomes blunted.

Social Class

Another factor that weakens the liberal prophetic voice is the tension between religious liberalism's prophetic impulse and the realities of its social location. In the biblical tradition, prophets could come from any sector of society, from the socially empowered establishment to the marginalized and socially devalued groups.[64] Today's social prophets may also appear from a variety of social locations. But it is difficult for someone from the social and economically privileged classes to speak effectively on behalf of the poor and powerless—an issue the biblical prophets confronted as well. Some scholars argue that in ancient Israel, the establishment prophets were more conservative than those on the periphery and that they tended to prefer gradual social change over radical social restructuring.[65]

Historically, religious liberals have come largely from the educated middle and upper-middle classes, and data from recent surveys confirm this.[66] In other words, religious liberals often belong to the very establishment they seek to critique. This is not necessarily an inconsistency. All members of a particular social class do not think alike, and even society's most privileged members are often critical of each other, as today's dysfunctional political climate clearly demonstrates. Even the most centrally located biblical prophets often pronounced radical judgments against those in power. The privileged can be powerful allies of the marginalized, but they need to be clear about whose agenda they are advancing and whose needs they are promoting.

H. R. Niebuhr's early insights into the link between denominationalism and social class are still worth noting, though today this link is less likely to reflect denominational categories.[67] In Niebuhr's view, middle-class churches tend to emphasize personal self-fulfillment and an ethic of individual responsibility, an orientation aimed more at satisfying the needs of the comfortable than the needs of the poor.[68] His analysis of these class issues led him later to conclude that religious liberals "are missionaries to the aristocracy and the middle-class."[69] While Niebuhr delivered this critique more than half a century ago, contemporary commentators have charged in similar terms that liberal theology serves as "an ideology for the bourgeois"[70] and that it often "ends up sanctioning the power structures of modern society."[71]

This critical assessment has not come only from the outside. A tradition of self-critique has always been an important part of religious liberalism, and liberals have long been aware of the impact of class. In the early 1940s, James Luther Adams criticized the neglect of prophetic faith among religious liberals, who instead offered what he called "religious sanction for the interests of a 'respectable' group."[72] This practice of critical self-examination continues today. A recurring theme in the work of

Unitarian Universalist ethicist Sharon Welch, for example, is the need for religious liberals to understand how their social location can interfere with a sustained commitment to social justice work.[73]

Yet self-critique alone cannot address the class tensions that affect liberalism's prophetic practice. Liberal religion's long association with the social and economic establishment has limited its ability to engage social justice concerns at a deep level, because overturning the existing system would be contrary to its own interests. The values of middle-class religion can easily tip the balance toward liberalism's cultural impulse and away from the prophetic. If liberals are to engage effectively in prophetic practice, we must acknowledge these class tensions and be alert to the ways they can inhibit this practice. In the end, we must realize that we always speak from our own social location, whatever our intentions about speaking on behalf of others.

Open-Ended Faith Commitments

The liberal commitment to free religious inquiry creates another tension that can interfere with liberal prophetic practice. This theological stance gives rise to flexible faith commitments and an open-ended approach to religious truth claims. Liberalism's principled theological openness is one of its great strengths. It is rooted in a commitment to intellectual honesty that Welch calls the "hallmark of liberal theology at its best."[74] This commitment forms the basis for the liberal tradition of constructive self-critique as well as liberalism's easy acceptance of theological diversity. Historically, it has reduced the importance and frequency of doctrinal disputes among religious liberals.

At the same time, this open-endedness contributes to a liberal tendency to hold religious commitments with a certain tentativeness. This does not mean that liberals have no religious convictions or at best only shallow convictions. Instead, it means that they are aware that religious faith, both individual and communal, evolves over time, and that the search for religious truth and meaning is never done. Nevertheless, this tendency toward open-endedness has its downside. Some religious liberals are reluctant to embrace the kind of clear theological commitments needed to ground a strong prophetic voice. Ironically, liberalism's openness seems to be accompanied by a tendency toward insularity. The reluctance to make firm religious commitments can lead to a kind of intellectual retreat that silences the liberal public voice and diminishes liberalism's influence in the public sphere.[75] This insularity may help explain the survey data showing the low level of support among religious liberals for having their religious leaders speak out on public issues.[76]

Theological Diversity

A fourth tension emerges from the broad range of theological perspectives found within religious liberalism. Diversity is a product of liberalism's theological openness, visible not only across the liberal spectrum but even within particular communities and congregations. Some of the more liberal denominations, such as Unitarian Universalists and Quakers, do not have creeds or sets of specific beliefs to which their members must subscribe. Individual congregations in these traditions often include everyone from Christian theists to neo-pagans to atheistic humanists. Even mainline Protestant churches normally include members who have a broad range of beliefs about the Bible, Jesus, and God. While these differences vary from congregation to congregation, religious liberals as a whole have always been relatively comfortable with this diversity. At its best, theological diversity is mutually enriching and helps create a welcoming atmosphere in liberal congregations.

Yet this diversity contains a tension that inhibits the liberal prophetic voice in much the same way as liberalism's open-endedness. Religious liberals tend to see their theological diversity as an expression of freedom of conscience and individual autonomy. While liberals encourage each other in their personal searches for truth and meaning, they often avoid making communal affirmations or even discussing their theological differences for fear of excluding or disrespecting other views. The result is that liberals easily fall prey to the current cultural tendency to see religious faith as a commodity to shop for, ironically devaluing the very faith claims they are seeking to welcome.

The search for truth can easily be seen as a threat to the very tolerance that invites it. Individual members may be subtly discouraged from searching too deeply and from publicly proclaiming their own beliefs with too much conviction. United Church of Christ minister and theologian Christopher Hinkle notes that "the 'rules' of interfaith dialogue generally preclude questions as to which of two competing doctrines seems most credible."[77] This is reflected in the sort of polite tolerance of theological diversity we often see in our congregations. The result is that many liberals have unwittingly adopted a kind of theological don't ask, don't tell policy. Fearful of saying something that might offend someone, we can easily end up saying nothing at all.

This tendency also appears in the liberal middle-class preference for rational and non-confrontational forms of public debate. In today's highly charged political and media climate, in which so-called debates have little substance and both candidates and commentators express themselves in pre-packaged high-volume sound bites, reflective religious liberals have difficulty finding room for their voices.

This problem is compounded by two additional tensions within religious liberalism. The first emerges from the ongoing debate about the proper role of religion in the public square, especially the claim by some liberal political philosophers that people should not support their positions on public issues with religious justifications. The second stems from religious liberals' long-standing commitment to the separation of church and state. These topics are complex and controversial, and the following chapters will examine their impact on religious liberalism in detail.

Liberal Religion and
Public Discourse

RELIGIOUS LIBERALS are among the most active faith-based advocates for social justice, in spite of their relative withdrawal from public consciousness over the past few decades. Liberals' discomfort with public religious discourse has meant that much of their social justice work is not done, publicly at least, in religious terms. Unfortunately, this habit of disguising religious commitments can weaken liberal prophetic practice. The goal of this chapter—indeed, a central goal of this book—is to help make liberal prophetic practice more effective by encouraging religious liberals to engage social justice issues more intentionally *as religious actors.* To do so, we need to get past our prejudice that speaking religiously in public is something that proper liberals just don't do.

Some examples may help illustrate the problem. I recently surveyed more than thirty resolutions adopted by the Unitarian Universalist Association—among the most liberal American religious groups—relating to issues of war and peace dating back to the creation of the UUA in 1961. Most read like political policy platforms rather than statements of religious conviction. None offered any theological grounding; fewer than 20 percent mentioned Unitarian Universalism's core Principles, and then only in passing among the introductory "whereas" clauses.

A 1964 General Resolution urging reconsideration of U.S. policy in Vietnam is typical. It reads in its entirety as follows:

WHEREAS, the political and military situation in South Vietnam is steadily deteriorating; and

WHEREAS, the danger of enlargement of the present war into a multi-national conflict is ominously increasing; and

WHEREAS, the intent of the Geneva Conference of 1954 was to neutralize the whole Indochinese peninsula;

THEREFORE BE IT RESOLVED: That we urge the United States government to reconsider its policy in Vietnam and to explore solutions other than military; and

BE IT FURTHER RESOLVED: That we urge the United States government to express its wish to participate in a reconvened Geneva Conference to consider the demilitarization and neutralization, under international guarantees, of Cambodia, Laos, and Vietnam.[78]

Note that the resolution is explained in terms of the political and military situation, but does not refer to any religious or moral values. The same basic approach is followed in a 1983 General Resolution opposing U.S. intervention in Nicaragua, a 1986 General Resolution urging U.S. compliance with the Strategic Arms Limitations Treaty, a 1995 Resolution of Immediate Witness condemning atrocities against civilians in Bosnia, a 2005 Action of Immediate Witness calling for an end to the crisis in Darfur, and many others.[79]

A 1991 Resolution calling for the lifting of nonmilitary sanctions against Iraq is typical of those that refer to one or more of the UUA Principles. It reads in part as follows:

WHEREAS we believe in the inherent worth and dignity of every person; . . .

WHEREAS the United States and Allied forces destroyed the infrastructure of Iraq, killed tens of thousands of people, left the people of Iraq without clean water, electricity, food and medical supplies, and thereby caused extreme public health and environmental problems . . .[80]

It refers to the Unitarian Universalist Principle affirming the inherent worth and dignity of all persons and notes the suffering caused by U.S. actions, but specifically linking the two by arguing that the actions violated this Principle would have made the resolution much stronger.

This pattern is followed in resolutions on other topics as well. One of the most recent, a 2011 Action of Immediate Witness in support of striking supermarket workers in Southern California, begins by quoting the Unitarian Universalist Principles affirming "the inherent worth and dignity of every person" and "justice, equity and compassion in human relations," and notes the denomination's long history of opposing racism and sexism.[81] It continues with ten "whereas" clauses reciting a range of social and economic data that demonstrates the injustice of the situation. This data is important; it explains why this action was thought to be necessary and helps argue for its passage. A case can easily be made that the situation described in these clauses violates a range of moral and religious norms relating to human worth and dignity, fair and equal treatment, concern for those least well-off, and love of one's neighbor, among others. Yet no such case is presented. While statements of this type add the Unitarian Universalist voice to the public debate, their largely secular, political tone means that they rarely offer a new or unique perspective on the issues. If the UUA proclaims little or no theological ground-ing for its position, why should it as a *religious* body take up this issue or adopt this particular stance? The same question can be asked about the many resolutions that do not even cite the Principles.

A major step in a new direction was taken with the UUA's 2010 Statement of Conscience on Creating Peace.[82] This state-ment includes a thorough presentation of the theological princi-ples and historical practices in which it is grounded, articulated not simply as abstract principles but in language that relates them specifically to the issue of peace. The theological affirmation of the fundamental unity and interdependence of all existence, for example, is expressed this way:

> The interdependence we have long affirmed has become the daily reality of our globalized world. Our interdependence makes it both possible and necessary that we see the peoples of the world as one community in which the security of each nation is entwined with the security of all others.

The statement also includes theological commitments relat-ing to human freedom, the transforming power of love, and the use of cooperative rather than coercive power, among others. Several of these commitments reach beyond the themes of the UUA Principles. For example, religious liberals have historically rejected the kind of moral dualism that artificially sets up rigid categories of good and evil. This theological conviction is articu-lated in language that speaks directly to the statement's peace theme:

> We reject as false the sharp separation of good and evil, refusing to assign individuals and nations into one category or the other.

Moral dualism can blind us to our own and our nation's capacity for evil and to the inherent worth and dignity of those whom our nation labels as enemies.

Regrettably, the 2010 Statement of Conscience is an exception; the general tendency to avoid religious language in UUA resolutions continues.

Part of the problem is historical and relates to what we might call religious style. The earliest forms of American religious liberalism were shaped in part by their opposition to the intensely emotional revivalism of the Great Awakening during the 1730s and 1740s. These early liberals rejected highly emotional religious expressions. Their roots in the Enlightenment inspired a more reserved and rational approach. For example, in his well-known 1742 sermon "Enthusiasm Described and Caution'd Against," liberal Boston congregationalist minister Charles Chauncy criticized the revivalists' disregard of reason and their display of "false and misleading emotions."[83] This attitude was not shared by all liberals of the time; early Universalists were often known for their religious enthusiasm. And even the more rationally inclined liberals did not question the importance of emotional religious experience.

Liberals have long found inward experience to lie at the heart of human religiousness.[84] A contemporary expression of this idea is found in the Unitarian Universalist Statement of Principles, which names "direct experience of that transcending mystery and wonder, affirmed in all cultures, which moves us to a renewal of the spirit and an openness to the forces which create and uphold life" as the first of its Sources.[85] Many liberal churches today have adopted more emotionally expressive forms of worship.[86] Yet a lingering discomfort with outward religious expression remains.

Religious liberals today may also be reluctant to speak religiously in public contexts because they don't want to seem "too religious." Over the past quarter century, the most visible and vocal religious groups in the United States have been those of the religious right. Many of these groups aggressively link conservative or fundamentalist theologies to conservative political agendas that liberals rightly perceive as creating threats to basic liberties, including religious liberty.[87] Religious liberals can all too easily buy into the widespread but erroneous assumption that if you're religious, you must be conservative. Religious liberals understandably want to avoid being perceived as conservative, so they keep quiet about their faith. Also, the liberal commitment to religious pluralism and free religious inquiry encourages religious liberals to avoid even the appearance of proselytizing, which they may associate with conservative evangelicalism. Similarly, religious liberals may associate religious public discourse with narrow-minded belligerence and want to avoid being associated with that.

These factors are an important part of the story, but over the past quarter century, a more subtle and potentially more inhibiting influence on liberal prophetic practice has appeared: the ongoing debate around the proper role of religion in public life. This debate is rooted in conflicting understandings of liberal political philosophy. It is important for religious liberals because we are heirs of the philosophical tradition that separates religion and politics. Some people think that this tradition requires not only the institutional separation of church and state but also a kind of intellectual separation of religious ideas and political deliberation. Several prominent political philosophers continue to hold up a secularized public square as the ideal and argue that religious arguments do not belong in public discourse. This position is generally taken to be the "liberal" view, so some religious liberals endorse it as part of their commitment to church-state separation or for other reasons. The danger is that delegitimizing public religious discourse encourages religious liberals to disguise their religious commitments and rationalizes their reluctance to speak publicly using religious language, thus undermining both the clarity and the conviction of their message, and in turn weakening the liberal prophetic voice.

This philosophical debate does not take place in a vacuum but is driven by several factors. First, our society is religiously and morally pluralistic. This may seem obvious but is worth stating because the central philosophical problem around which the larger debate revolves is usually framed in terms of pluralism. Philosopher John Rawls frames the question well: "How is it possible that there may exist over time a stable and just society of free and equal citizens profoundly divided by reasonable though incompatible religious, philosophical, and moral doctrines?[88]

Our moral pluralism results in different visions of what constitutes a good society, and this affects our ability to carry on constructive public dialogue. Roman Catholic theologian John Courtney Murray noted a half century ago that "civil discourse would be hard enough if among us there prevailed conditions of religious unity."[89] But we do not share a common moral language, so we cannot take for granted that other participants in public discussion share our basic social values and moral reference points. As a result, groups can easily misunderstand each other's messages and may distrust each other's motives. Under these conditions, it is remarkable that we can talk to each other at all.

Second, religion has always been part of American public life, and historically, most people believed that it should be. The nation's founders, while insisting on separation of church and state, nevertheless believed that religion played an important role in the development of civic responsibility and maintaining a morally healthy society.[90] This view was shared by early liberal religious leaders such as William Ellery Channing, who spoke of the "importance of religion to society."[91] Religious groups are as publicly visible and politically active today as they have ever been. For most political philosophers, political involvement is not the problem. Those who say that religiously grounded arguments do not belong in public discourse are not claiming that religious people should simply stay home. Rather, they argue that when religious people do get involved, they should not make distinctly religious arguments. Instead, they should speak in the common language of rational secular discourse.

Third, much of what faith communities say and do has important public or political implications. By the same token, many public issues have moral implications of the type that faith communities routinely address. Faith communities, then, have the potential to enrich the public dialogue. Religious groups may more likely be concerned with conveying their message effectively than with conforming to a particular philosophical position. But the underlying positions matter because they can influence how religious communities understand their place in a pluralistic democratic society. The heritage of political liberalism makes this especially true for religious liberals.

The debate in political philosophy is not about whether religious voices should speak, but how. Should special rules apply to those who justify their social and political positions on religious grounds? Liberal political philosophers who prefer a more holistic and inclusive form of liberalism increasingly challenge those who would exclude religious justifications. This is an encouraging development. Including religiously grounded arguments in public debate is philosophically justifiable, consistent with the First Amendment, and in accord with liberal values. In fact, seeking to exclude religious arguments is distinctly *illiberal*. The alternative perspective welcomes religious voices as equal public dialogue partners. It is, in other words, fully compatible with the concerns of both religious and political liberalism.

The Debate

There is no shortage of material surrounding this philosophical debate, which has been carried on in dozens of books, hundreds of academic and nonacademic articles, blogs, columns, and other forums over the past two decades. Positions have been articulated and refined, challenged and defended at great length, and new contributions appear every year. The subtle distinctions among all the philosophical arguments need not be addressed in detail. From the perspective of religious liberals engaged in prophetic practice, the questions are straightforward. In a pluralistic democracy, is it proper for the liberal prophetic voice to speak in specifically religious terms? Or does being a good democratic citizen—and a good religious liberal—mean that we should bracket our religious views and make our public case using non-religious forms of justification? Finally, which approach generates the most effective prophetic practice?

From these crucial questions, the debate comes down to two basic positions. The first holds that religious reasons do not belong in public discourse. Instead, citizens in a pluralistic democracy should state their positions in terms of a neutral "public reason," whose norms and modes of discourse are shared by all. This position is known as the separatist view, the translation model, the exclusionist approach, or simply as political liberalism. The alternative position challenges the assumption that religion should be kept out of the public square. It holds that religiously grounded arguments should be welcome in public discourse, even when citizens bring widely different and often conflicting background assumptions and core values to the table. This perspective is called the integrationist approach, the conversation model, and the inclusionist approach.[92]

Before looking more closely at these two approaches and their effect on liberal prophetic practice, we may ask how the exclusionist approach came to be understood as the "liberal" position. What can possibly be liberal about wanting to exclude any viewpoint from public dialogue? To begin, it helps to understand that the central concern of liberal political theory is the fairness of political process. Political liberals focus on process rather than content because our radical religious and moral pluralism makes agreeing on content — on what makes for a good society — extremely unlikely. The best we can do is to set up fair ground rules so that everyone gets to participate as equally as possible. To ensure the fairness of public discourse, political liberals emphasize two core democratic values: the tradition of *reason-giving*, and the principle of *accessibility*.

Reason-Giving

One of the core practices of participatory democracy is a commitment to a form of public discussion that includes giving reasons for our views. Democratic dialogue is not simply about expressing our opinions and preferences; we are expected to justify our positions by showing how and why we reached them. Philosopher and ethicist Jeffrey Stout argues that this principle lies at the very heart of democracy. Citizens may be divided on any number of important issues, but "one thing [they] had better have in common is . . . a way of exchanging reasons about ethical and political topics." This practice is "where the life of democracy principally resides."[93]

The practice of reason-giving is deeply engrained in our political culture. One of our great models is the Declaration of Independence. Its premise is that when a group of people is about to take the radical step of separating themselves, they are obliged to explain why. Its familiar language reads:

> When in the course of human events, it becomes necessary for one people to dissolve the political bands which have connected them with another . . . a decent respect to the opinions of mankind requires that they should declare the causes which impel them to the separation.

The remainder of the Declaration consists almost entirely of a list of reasons. Philosophical and theological principles—propositions the signers held to be self-evident but nevertheless articulated carefully—are followed by a long list of specific grievances against the king. Only after having made their case do they declare their independence and disavow their allegiance to the British crown.

Political philosophers Amy Gutmann and Dennis Thompson argue that the practice of reason-giving rests on the moral principle of mutual respect: "Citizens show respect to one another by recognizing their obligation to justify to one another . . . the laws and policies that govern their public life."[94] People may disagree on the policies, and they may not think much of each other's reasons. But the fact that we respect each other enough to explain the reasons for our views is a kind of civic moral glue that helps hold the community together in spite of our disagreements. The practice of public reason-giving also contains a built-in mechanism for accountability. Those who make decisions that affect our lives are accountable not only for their decisions but also for the justifications they give. When political leaders make policy decisions behind closed doors, or when the reasons they give fly in the face of the facts, they not only violate the core values of democratic discourse, but they also undermine public faith in democracy itself.

Prophetic religious practice is fully in tune with this democratic tradition. Even the biblical prophets did not simply pronounce God's judgment on the targets of their criticism. They identified specific shortcomings and failures, often in some detail. The people worshipped false gods; the wealthy trampled the poor; the leaders no longer listened to the people. The examples from the Unitarian Universalist Association cited above follow the same reason-giving practice. In terms of liberal political theory, the problem is not with the practice of giving reasons; it is with the kinds of reasons given. Here the principle of accessibility comes into play.

Accessibility

The liberal emphasis on fair process means that we must find a way to speak about public issues that enables us to understand each other. Many political liberals think we should use forms of argument that are, in principle at least, accessible to everyone. As Gutmann and Thompson explain, "To justify imposing their will on you, your fellow citizens must give reasons that are comprehensible to you. If you seek to impose your will on them, you owe them no less."[95] Some political philosophers see this principle as the problem with religious justifications. An argument is not accessible if it is stated in terms that cannot reasonably be evaluated by others, or as legal philosopher Kent Greenawalt puts it, if "the believer lacks bases to show others the truth of what he believes."[96]

From this perspective, arguments that rely on personal religious experience or divine revelation are neither accessible nor authoritative to those outside a particular tradition. They may not even be comprehensible, let alone capable of being evaluated or rebutted. Arguments grounded in justifications available only to a particular individual or group are in this sense undemocratic. Political liberals in the exclusionist camp want to keep this sort of religious justification out of public discourse. Summarizing the views of a few key figures will provide a sense of how religious liberals are affected by this debate.

Among the most extreme exclusionary positions is that of political philosopher Bruce Ackerman, who argues that religious justifications should not be permitted because they are based on a worldview not shared by others, and therefore amount to a claim of privileged moral authority. For Ackerman, "nobody has the right to vindicate political authority by asserting a privileged insight into the moral universe which is denied the rest of us."[97] Instead, dialogue must be based on shared moral values. Yet our vast religious and moral pluralism means that it will not always be possible to find a shared moral framework. Ackerman argues that when this happens, we should not bother looking for common ground, nor should we try to translate our positions into some form of neutral language. Instead, "we should simply say *nothing at all* about this disagreement and put the moral ideals that divide us off the conversational agenda of the liberal state."[98] Philosopher Richard Rorty takes a similar position, claiming that in the democratic public square, religion is a "conversation stopper."[99] The practical effect of this position is to shut off public conversation altogether among persons who hold different sets of religious or moral values. This result is hardly acceptable in a democratic society, and this position could not be endorsed by inclusivist-minded religious liberals. In fact, by the terms of his own argument, Ackerman's position would seem to be the real conversation stopper.[100]

Greenawalt's views lie roughly in the middle of the exclusion-ist spectrum. He rejects the liberal dogma that citizens in a liberal democratic society should not rely on their religious convictions when making political choices. He is well aware that people's religious beliefs influence not only their personal ethical choices but also their positions on government policies and laws. As a result, there is no good reason to require that religious convic-tions take a back seat to non-religious convictions. Yet Greenawalt draws a curious distinction between the process of formulating one's political choices and the process of publicly articulating or justifying them. It is perfectly proper, he says, for religious people to rely on their religious beliefs as they think through issues and come to conclusions. But when it comes to open discussion or public advocacy, the religious citizen should not make explicitly religious arguments. Instead, she should make her arguments "in essentially non-religious terms."[101]

Making a distinction between forming one's views and pub-licly articulating them is problematic for several reasons. The most important is that it misunderstands the nature of human decision making. Perhaps political philosophers can neatly iden-tify and compartmentalize their own internal blend of reasoned analysis, value judgments, emotional needs, and other elements— including religious beliefs—and come to clear conclusions that they then translate into suitably secular language. But I suspect that most of our minds do not work in this way. Indeed, the pro-cess suggested by Greenawalt seems artificial and even a little dishonest, especially for people with deeply held religious convictions. Thus, while Greenawalt is clearly more sympathetic to religiously motivated public discourse than Ackerman, he ends up in the same exclusionist place.

The opposite end of the spectrum is represented by John Rawls, whose widely discussed 1993 book *Political Liberalism* has influenced the course of this debate perhaps more than any other single work.[102] Rawls's central concern is how a society made up of people and groups with widely divergent religious and moral views can nevertheless agree on the basic principles needed to form a stable democracy. He assumes that no one group can do so because its particular views might not be shared by others and because doing so would privilege the values of that group. The philosophical basis for a constitutional democracy, therefore, must be one that can be endorsed by a broad range of groups with different and sometimes conflicting religious and moral perspectives. The common space created by this mutual endorsement is what Rawls calls the "overlapping consensus," and political discourse takes place within this space.

Rawls argues that when we participate in this public space, whether or not we are religious believers, we should think of ourselves as citizens and not as members of groups with religious or other particular identities. Thus, when we engage in public political discussion with others who may not share our particular views, we should use a form of argument Rawls calls "public reason." Rawls says that "we are not to appeal to comprehensive religious and philosophical doctrines—to what we as individuals or members of associations see as the whole truth." Instead, our justifications should "rest on the plain truths now widely accepted, or available, to citizens generally."[103] In other words, people should not make specifically religious arguments in public political discourse.

Although his position is exclusivist, Rawls blunts its impact by arguing that the limitations of public reason do not apply to all types of public political discussion, but only to those that involve what he calls "constitutional essentials" and "questions of basic justice."[104] These deal with the most basic elements of any democracy, such as the powers of the various branches of government; the basic rights and liberties of citizenship, including the right to vote and freedom of thought and association; and the protections of the rule of law. Debate on these issues must follow the principles of public reason. But debate on other issues, such as legislation dealing with regulation of property and industry or funding of social programs, for example, would be free of these restraints. In these contexts, according to Rawls, religiously grounded arguments are perfectly proper.

He later added a now-famous *proviso* to his original principle of public reason, further opening the door to public religious arguments. Under the proviso, religious citizens may base public arguments on their own religious views at any time, even on the core political issues, "provided that in due course proper political reasons . . . are presented that are sufficient to support whatever the [religious views] are said to support."[105] In other words, religious arguments are perfectly acceptable in all types of public discourse. But when the debate involves core democratic principles, those who make religious argument should be prepared to restate them in non-religious terms. Rawls also says that the presence of religious arguments in public discussions can have a positive value because, for many citizens, allegiance to democracy is rooted in their deepest religious convictions. If they see that their unique views are acceptable in public discourse, their commitment to the principle of public reason will be strengthened.

For Rawls, then, religious views are welcome in public debate. At the same time, he always has one eye on the realities of pluralism, which makes him wary of relying on religious justifications alone for the core constitutional and political structures. In this context, the principle of public reason becomes a form of protection against the threat of theocracy: "While no one is expected to put his or her religious or non-religious doctrine in danger, we must each give up forever the hope of changing the constitution so as to establish our religion's hegemony."[106]

Most political theorists who object to public religious arguments rely heavily on the accessibility factor. Many of them seem to assume that religious convictions are always grounded in supernatural or mystical sources that lie beyond the reach of reason, or in texts or institutions whose authority is limited to particular groups.[107] This unfortunately narrow view of religion does not describe liberal religion. Prophetic practice grounded and expressed in the principles of liberal religion will almost always satisfy the democratic principle of accessibility. A central methodological criterion of liberal theology is the conviction that theological claims must be intelligible to and consistent with other areas of human knowledge. And liberal religion's basic cultural orientation pushes it toward shared reference points. This means that religious liberals will tend to articulate their religious convictions in ways others will understand. Once political philosophers get past their prejudice that religious views are inherently inaccessible, they should recognize that liberal prophetic practice will be acceptable to most versions of liberal political theory, even when that critique is stated in religious terms. For this reason, even the exclusionist version of political liberalism does not justify religious liberals' reluctance to speak publicly using religious language.

An Alternative Liberalism

Making the case for liberal prophetic practice in terms of traditional liberal political theory leaves the exclusionist positions in place and argues that we should be counted among the privileged voices who get to play the public reason game. Liberal prophetic practice would be better off if we stopped worrying about satisfying these particular philosophical demands and simply spoke the language of our own religious convictions. Fortunately, an alternative inclusivist view of political liberalism supports this stance. A growing number of political theorists now argue that political liberalism need not—and should not—exclude religious reasons from public argument, even if those reasons are not fully accessible in the traditional sense.

One of the more interesting positions in this regard is that of moral philosopher and legal scholar Michael Perry. Early on in this debate, Perry wrote two books in which he aligned himself with the exclusionists. He argued that religious arguments in public discourse were proper only if they satisfied the conditions of public accessibility and did not rely on sources or modes of reasoning that had no authority outside one's own religious group.[108] Perry has now abandoned this position and joined the inclusionist camp. Significantly, his current view on religious discourse begins with the core values of liberal democracy, which he identifies as a "commitment to the true and full humanity of every person" and an "allied commitment to certain basic human freedoms." He argues that nothing in these core values makes it "illegitimate for religious believers to introduce religiously grounded moral belief into public political argument."[109]

Perry is aware that religion can be sectarian and divisive, but this is also true of secular modes of discourse. Besides, he says, in a country as religious as the United States, trying to exclude religious voices makes no sense. He does not mean that religious perspectives should be free from challenge. Once these perspectives enter the public debate, others may criticize their conclusions and justifications. By the same token, religious people are free to challenge the positions and reasoning of other groups, both religious and non-religious. Prophetic religious practice often involves precisely this kind of challenge. But the participation of religious groups is not undemocratic. Perry concludes that "in a liberal democracy, it is altogether fitting—it is altogether 'liberal'—for religious believers to make political choices . . . on the ground of what is, for them, a religious claim."[110]

Perry is not alone; many political philosophers have articulated similar views. Political philosopher Christopher Eberle, for example, argues that a citizen should be "morally permitted to support (or oppose) a coercive law even if he has only a religious rationale."[111] Religious citizens should not completely disregard the kinds of reasons used by others; they have an obligation to at least try to state their own reasons in more broadly based terms. But in the end they can still join the discussion even if they have only religious reasons. Philosopher J. Caleb Clanton agrees. He says flatly that religious citizens, like non-religious citizens, "are free to employ whatever reasons they see fit to advance in the course of public deliberation."[112] In doing so, they run the risk that these arguments may be challenged for being incoherent, for contradicting the available evidence, for reaching conclusions not supported by their own premises, or for other reasons. But the same is true for secular arguments, so that is no reason to exclude them. Finally, Jeffrey Stout argues that when citizens express the reasons they actually have, religious or otherwise, they show each other the respect required in a democracy. In this way, "each person's deepest commitments can be recognized for what they are and assessed accordingly."[13]

This development is encouraging for several reasons. First, it corresponds to reality. Religious people have been giving religious reasons for their positions in the American public dialogue since the beginning—and this is not likely to change soon. Our increased pluralism may make dialogue more difficult today, but that is a reason to include diverse views, not to exclude those that don't easily conform to the dominant mode of discourse. In this regard, the exclusionist view has implications not only for religious views but also for other nonmainstream orientations— especially those of women, recent immigrants, and persons of color.

Second, the inclusionist position is more honest and therefore more respectful. It encourages people to say what they really mean, rather than being forced to disguise their commitments or translate them into language that is foreign to them and risks distorting their meaning. Third, religious people have much to contribute. Most public issues have moral implications that faith communities deal with all the time, and their voices can enrich the public discussion. Fourth, the inclusionist view abandons the prejudice that religious claims are inherently suspect and therefore can't be trusted. This does not mean that religiously based reasons or any other kinds of reasons are beyond criticism. It may well be that some religious beliefs are based on bad theology or inadequate reasoning or faulty premises. If so, we may point this out in our response to them. Likewise, if religious people make public arguments that are inaccessible in the sense discussed earlier, that is something to consider when judging their relevance or persuasiveness. This is all the more reason to encourage people to give their real reasons.

Finally, excluding religious voices contributes to the shallowness of our public discourse. A philosophical position insisting that we all speak in some allegedly neutral common language simply "ensures that our discourse will often be barren, unsatisfying, and shallow"[14] as legal scholar Steven Smith puts it.

As religious liberals, we don't have to buy into the exclusionist account of political liberalism, the view that wants to standardize public political discourse and keep religion safely tucked away in our private closets. We can use religious language in our prophetic practice, give religious reasons in our statements on public issues, and still be good liberals.

What Does It Mean to Speak Religiously?

My claim that liberal prophetic practice would be strength-ened if religious liberals were more intentional about their reli-gious grounding raises an obvious but important question: What does it mean to speak religiously? This is not a simple question. Most of us do not carefully compartmentalize our thoughts and speech. When we speak on public issues, as when we speak in private contexts, our motivations, our guiding moral convictions, and even our choices of language normally reflect a complex blend of many interrelated factors. In addition to intellectual factors such as our analysis of the relevant issues, there are also psychological and emotional factors, cultural influences and group pressures, and personal preferences. Our religious convic-tions form an important part of this jumble, but we cannot always separate them or determine which of these diverse elements has priority.

For example, as religious liberals, we are committed to the values of social justice, human freedom, and shared power in decision making. But you don't have to be a religious liberal to hold these values; they are among the core values of liberal democracy and thus widely shared in our society. Moreover, our commitment to these values likely was formed through a combi-nation of influences. Religious teachings may be among them, but learning from our teachers, families, and friends; the influence of books, films and television; the role played by police or gangs or helpful neighbors during our childhoods; and many other factors affect the way we come to understand concepts such as freedom, justice, and power. If I now claim, as an adult who identifies as a religious liberal, that a government policy is unjust or that a legislative proposal would impinge on human freedom, am I making a religious argument, a political argument, or something else? It is often impossible to distinguish. Yet my claim that religious liberals should speak more religiously on public issues apparently asks us to make this very distinction.

For religious liberals the problem is complicated by our unwillingness to compartmentalize the religious and non-religious dimensions of our lives. The liberal tradition of expressing religious convictions in light of contemporary knowledge and experience is a related factor. We are likely to have both religious and non-religious reasons for our positions on particular issues, and we might choose to emphasize one or another for strategic or other reasons. In most cases, we will likely seek to blend these different voices and motivations. This practice can be effective, but it is important that we not allow our religious motivations to disappear into our cultural identity or our political preferences. If our religion plays a significant role in our lives, then it must do more than simply reinforce the values of our culture. In fact, despite the liberal preference for intentional engagement with the larger culture, our religious values are often deeply countercultural. Articulating the ways these values challenge certain cultural ideas about wealth accumulation and personal responsibility, for example, is part of what it means to be prophetic. According to religious ethicist Robin Lovin:

More fully developed religious ideas do not simply replicate cultural notions of personal satisfaction. They enrich our sense of the possibilities life offers, extend our concerns to people and places we have heretofore ignored, and transform our sense of what would make us happy by showing us ways of life that our own limited experience could not devise. Both for believers themselves and for others, the public articulation of religious reasons for action provides images of human good that may be attractive and persuasive, even (or especially) when they differ from the usual ideas of happiness and fulfillment.[115]

Lovin's observation applies as much to religious liberals as to other religious groups. Our vision of a just society, for example, is informed by many sources, but our religious convictions play a major role. This vision informs the positions we take on public issues, and articulating our positions in light of this vision adds weight to our prophetic message and enriches the public dialogue. Unlike the biblical prophets, we cannot assume that those to whom our words and deeds are directed share our religious and moral reference points or our understanding of such core values as equality, freedom, and justice. Other participants in the public dialogue won't know where we are coming from unless we tell them.

What can this mean in practice? At a minimum, religious liberals need to be clearer and more intentional about the religious dimensions of our convictions. We can look at our complex tangle of motivations and try to discern how our religious commitments fit. We can say to ourselves, "Yes, my commitment to social justice is based at least partly on my religious convictions," and then try to express them in ways that address specific situations. We might oppose a particular proposal for immigration reform, for instance, not only because it is economically unjust or operates in a discriminatory manner, but also because it treats a particular group in a way that denies their inherent human worth and dignity.

When we speak publicly, we can be intentional about saying that there *are* religious reasons, and that they matter. Opposition to a proposed tax change that favors the wealthy, for example, might be expressed in several ways. The change could be opposed on non-religious public policy grounds by arguing that it imposes an unfair burden on the middle class or that it would contribute to economic instability. But the same position can be supported by religious values as well. We might say, "As a religious liberal (or as a concerned Christian or Unitarian Universalist or practicing Jew), I believe that justice requires us to be concerned primarily for those who have least. Since the policy you are proposing would favor those who have most, it is unjust." This statement honors the religious dimension of our identity while also bringing our liberal religious values into the public discussion.

To further illustrate these points, we can reconsider the 1964 Unitarian Universalist Resolution on Vietnam discussed in the previous chapter. This resolution urging the U.S. government to explore nonmilitary solutions to the Vietnam conflict was based entirely on a judgment about the deteriorating military situation and the danger of expanded war. It contained no religious language and therefore offered no clue as to why this particular stance should be taken by a liberal religious organization. How might the resolution have looked if its religious grounding had been made explicit? While rewriting it from a distance of nearly half a century would be impossible and unfair to those who passed it, we can nevertheless suggest that the following language might have clarified its religious grounding and added to its moral weight:

We affirm the cooperative use of power and the priority of non-violent conflict resolution, and the Vietnam conflict is no exception. Because U.S. military actions have failed to resolve the Vietnamese conflict and instead threaten to provoke a multinational war, we call on the United States government to reconsider its policy and to explore nonmilitary solutions.

Or,

As Unitarian Universalists, we affirm the inherent worth and dignity of every person, including those our government now labels as enemies, as well as a shared obligation to create just and stable political institutions that enable human fulfillment. Because continuation of present U.S. policy in Vietnam will bring further loss of human life and further destruction of the resources necessary to sustain just communities, we call on the United States government to abandon its present policy and to commit itself to a just resolution through nonmilitary means.

We can also examine a few recent examples of liberal prophetic public statements that do make effective use of religious justifications. One is a 2000 United Methodist Church Resolution calling for changes to the Illegal Immigration Reform and Immigrant Responsibility Act of 1996 and for the adoption of an amnesty program for undocumented immigrants. The resolution begins by clearly articulating its religious basis, noting that "the Holy Scriptures call us as the community of God to give shelter, protection and help to sojourners living amongst us, reminding us that we, too, were foreigners in other times." It then discusses the negative human consequences of unjust immigration enforcement, linking the biblical value of hospitality to international norms relating to immigration and human rights, and concludes that the 1996 law permitting these practices is "evil and unjust."[116]

Another helpful example is a 2011 United Church of Christ Resolution calling for the application of international human rights principles to protect against abuse or discrimination based on sexual orientation or gender identity. This resolution begins by explaining its biblical and theological rationale:

> The foundation of human rights derives from the creation narratives of scripture in which human beings are created by God in the image of God. In the Gospel of Matthew . . . Jesus exhorts his disciples to address the needs of the "least" that are hungry, thirsty, a stranger, naked, sick, or in prison. The Church acts faithfully when it regards all humans as equal in worth and dignity and when it seeks the just treatment of all in societies and by laws and public authorities.[17]

The resolution then links these theological convictions to the moral norms implicit in international human rights standards. It discusses how these norms are violated by instances of abuse and discrimination around the world and argues that the use of criminal law against members of sexual minorities violates both international human rights norms and these deep religious values.

While denominational resolutions offer one occasion for prophetic witness, another is making statements before public authorities, ranging from local school boards and town councils to state legislatures and congressional committees. In this regard, the 2006 statement by Rev. William Sinkford, then president of the Unitarian Universalist Association, to a group of congressional staffers offers an excellent example of effective liberal public prophetic witness grounded in clearly expressed religious convictions. Sinkford was speaking in opposition to a proposed Federal Marriage Amendment that would have prohibited same-sex marriage. He began by grounding his position in Unitarian

Universalist theological principles and collective liberal religious experience:

> Within Unitarian Universalism, we know from our own experience the many blessings that gay and lesbian people bring to our congregations and communities. We know from our lived experience in religious community that differences of faith, of race and of sexual orientation need not divide us, that diversity within the human family can be a blessing and not a curse. Unitarian Universalists affirm that it is the presence of love and commitment that we value. For Unitarian Universalists, it is homophobia that is the sin, not homosexuality. Unitarian Universalists Stand on the Side of Love.[118]

Sinkford then linked this deep religious conviction to public policy arguments about discrimination and personal freedom, noting the historical parallels between the proposed marriage amendment and earlier laws prohibiting interracial marriage.[119] These policy positions could have been stated independently, supported perhaps by principles drawn from political philosophy, sociological analysis, or constitutional law. But other advocates were already making these arguments, and without its religious grounding, Sinkford's statement would have added nothing to the public debate. By straightforwardly linking secular policies with religious justifications, he deepened his argument and likely reached a wider audience.

Sinkford's observations following a private meeting with members of Congress make a similar point. "Several members said that they had learned important things that affected their views on the amendment. Hearing religious arguments from religious leaders was particularly important."[120] And hearing *liberal* religious arguments from religious liberals is critical. We may hope that Sinkford's religious perspective broadened the legislators' understanding of the issue. At the very least, it gave them an alternative religious perspective that counterbalanced the arguments religious conservatives have long been making.

Another example illustrating effective and ineffective uses of religiously grounded arguments in a public venue took place in the 1980 hearings before the United States Congress on the so-called Helms Amendment.[121] This legislative proposal was a blatant attempt to undermine earlier Supreme Court rulings holding that officially sponsored prayer in public schools violated the Establishment Clause of the First Amendment.[122] The bill would have created space for school prayer by restricting the jurisdiction of the federal courts to hear prayer cases. More than a dozen religious organizations testified on this bill, about half on each side. Some based their support or opposition exclusively on secular public policy, with no mention of religion at all. Others, however, offered explicitly religious and theological arguments.

William Bright, founder and then president of Campus Crusade for Christ, a large and influential evangelical organization, presented the most uncompromising religious testimony in support of the proposal. Bright began by grounding his testimony in the theology of his particular tradition, noting his "firm belief that *God is*, and that He is as the Bible reveals Him." Bright made clear that he believed the United States is a divinely chosen people and that biblical principles should control matters of public policy, including public education. He also claimed that the Supreme Court's 1963 decision in *Abingdon v. Schempp*,[123] which outlawed mandatory Bible reading in public schools, offended God and "precipitated His chastening and judgment upon our land." Nearly all of the nation's problems since then, he said, were the direct consequences of that decision, including the

Vietnam War; the assassinations of John Kennedy, Robert Kennedy, and Martin Luther King Jr.; racial conflict in the cities; and teenage suicide. Bright asserted that these and other problems were "the modern equivalent of the plagues of Egypt" and would be reversed only when prayer and the Bible were returned to the public schools.[124]

What are we to make of this argument? First, it was based on particularistic religious reasoning that was not publicly accessible in the sense intended by liberal political philosophy. Bright made no attempt to state his position in terms that might communicate to those outside his own tradition. He clearly cared little for the pluralism of American society, which he specifically branded as evil, and he was not interested in any genuine public debate or dialogue. This does not mean that his testimony was illegitimate, although that would likely be the conclusion of those who adhere to the exclusionist philosophical position discussed in the previous chapter. But certainly, members of Congress and others should have taken into account his unusual forms of logic when evaluating the merits of his claims. The transparency of his religious language reveals the weaknesses of his argument even on its own terms. There is no moral reasoning, even from his own religious premises, and his statements are full of post hoc and other logical fallacies that most high-school debate students wouldn't make. In the end, his extreme religious views seem likely to have persuaded only those who already shared his position, and he ultimately contributed little to the larger public debate on the issue of prayer in schools.

While such statements may seem ludicrous to religious liberals, they cannot be ignored. We need not answer them on their own theological terms by arguing, for example, that his plague claim misinterprets the biblical story. But we make a huge mistake if we fail to challenge these sorts of public religious voices by offering an alternative religious perspective. John Houck, then general secretary of the Lutheran Council in the U.S.A., did just that. Houck was opposed to any form of school prayer and testified against the Helms Amendment.

Houck too began his public testimony with a clear theological position grounded in his Lutheran tradition: "Our position on school prayer reflects our theological presuppositions about prayer, an essential part of our religious life." He objected to non-denominational school prayer because it "conveys none of the substance, the depth, or the cutting edge of our historic witness." But Houck did not stop with theology. He used this theological position as the foundation to support his public policy arguments relating to education and individual rights. He argued that "prayer and religious readings in school classrooms [have] dubious value either as an educational or religious experience." He expressed concern that religious exercises in the public schools "may infringe on the rights of some individuals and groups in society and invite sectarian divisiveness in the community."[125] He also affirmed the importance of a uniform interpretation of the First Amendment throughout the country, something the proposed amendment would have prevented by shifting the venue for legal challenges to the state courts.

Like William Bright, Houck testified as a religious person. Unlike Bright, however, his statement carefully blended religious and non-religious arguments, giving it a depth that enriched its contribution to the debate. If he had omitted the religious arguments, his testimony would not only have been weaker, it would have added nothing to the arguments made by other witnesses testifying for secular organizations. If he had left the theological arguments to stand on their own, as Bright did, he would have effectively cut himself off from the larger debate. Unlike the Campus Crusaders, the Lutherans were willing to acknowledge that others who did not share their religious views were part of the conversation. Houck was able to address the public issues about school prayer in terms to which others could respond, but without abandoning his own theological grounding.

In these examples of liberal prophetic practice, the clearly articulated theological grounding of the public statements clarified why these groups felt called to adopt their positions *as religious liberals*. It also strengthened their appeal to other sources, such as international human rights norms, constitutional law, and political philosophy, by showing the deep relationship between religious liberalism and the underlying moral values expressed in these sources. The public expression of this relationship adds moral weight to the statements and thus contributes to the effectiveness of liberal prophetic practice.

Religious liberals need to reclaim our share of the public space. There is more to this than adopting resolutions and making public statements, of course. Prophetic witness also takes place through forms of direct action such as demonstrations, vigils, protests, and in other ways. But whatever the setting for specific prophetic practices, the liberal religious basis for undertaking them must be clearly and publicly named. Given the public dominance of conservative religious voices today, if religious liberals don't speak up, no one else will know that there is another religious perspective.

Religious Liberalism and Religious Freedom

RELIGIOUS FREEDOM, one of our most precious rights, is deeply engrained in our social and political culture. Religious groups across the theological spectrum, including religious liberals, share a long-standing commitment to religious freedom and to the principle of church-state separation, an important part of religious freedom as understood in the United States. Few people want an established or official church, or think we'd be better off if we all shared the same faith.[126]

While Americans broadly agree that religious freedom is a good thing, we don't all agree on what it means. It's not just that the law is unclear, though it is; Supreme Court decisions on the First Amendment's religion clauses are famously confused and inconsistent. But on a deeper level, we have different and often conflicting understandings of what sorts of practices should be permitted in the name of religion, the role the government should play in accommodating citizens' religious practices, the extent to which religious groups should influence public policy, and so on. Policies and laws that for some seem to protect religious freedom look to others like special privilege. Religious influence on public issues, which for some constitutes an important and deeply felt expression of faith, to others seems corrupting and coercive. Our political and theological starting points affect our views about these difficult issues.

Our views in turn affect the way we understand the role of prophetic practice. For religious liberals, the commitment to separation of church and state produces a tension that can interfere with liberal prophetic practice. On the surface, there seems to be a potential conflict between religious liberalism's commitment to church-state separation, on one hand, and its basic posture of cultural engagement on the other. Political scientist Laura Olson notes that a "very real mobilization problem . . . results when religious [leaders] vehemently argue that church and state should not be excessively entangled yet ask the people in the pews to take political action to address injustice."[127] In addition, some religious liberals mistakenly believe that church-state separation precludes the use of religious language in public discourse, or at least that speaking religiously on public issues somehow threatens this important constitutional value. Unfortunately, this misunderstanding of what church-state separation does and doesn't require reinforces the belief that religion should remain safely sequestered in the private sphere. Prophetic religious practice, in contrast, is necessarily an engaged and public form of religious exercise.

As noted earlier, religious liberals are less likely than members of other groups to participate in various forms of political activities or to support such activities by clergy and denominational leaders. This trend is reflected in data showing that religious liberals and mainline Protestants have become substantially less active in defending the First Amendment. Since 1990, these denominational groups have filed far fewer amicus curiae briefs in relevant Supreme Court cases, for example, and they have sharply curtailed their lobbying activities on congressional bills proposing such measures as school prayer amendments or public funding for religious schools.[128]

This decreased activity comes precisely as the Supreme Court has adopted an increasingly accommodationist view of the First Amendment's religion clauses. This approach has now largely displaced the so-called strict separation theory, which had been articulated most clearly during the 1960s in the public school prayer and Bible reading cases. Since 1990, the Court has been much more willing to uphold governmental support of religion against establishment challenges and legislative restrictions on religious activity against free exercise challenges.[129] Church-state scholar Derek Davis suggests that the religious mainline "has abdicated its historic role as the champion of the First Amendment."[130] This may simply be part of the larger trend of diminishing activism among religious liberals. As a practical matter, it probably also reflects reduced funding of denominational Washington offices.

Interestingly, the Supreme Court's shift in its approach to the First Amendment coincides with the liberal and mainline retrenchment in First Amendment advocacy. Religious liberals may have felt more secure in their activism when the Court followed a strict separation approach, and the boundary between church and state was more secure. As the metaphorical wall of separation increasingly erodes, liberals may fear that their public prophetic activities could contribute to the trend. And because the Supreme Court's accommodationist approach is supported by many activist religious conservatives, liberals may simply want to avoid being associated with this view. The result is that religious liberals fail to defend their commitment to religious liberty precisely when this defense is most needed.

Religious liberalism's dual commitments to separation of church and state and to active cultural and social engagement are not inconsistent. The liberal fear that public religious expression threatens church-state separation stems in part from a common misperception about the First Amendment. It is a basic principle of constitutional law that the First Amendment, like the rest of the Bill of Rights, operates as a restriction on the powers of the state, not on the actions of private individuals or groups. It protects fundamental rights and liberties by restricting the ability of the government to limit or deny them. Indeed, a law that prohibited religious people from participating in political activities or speaking on public issues would be a clear violation of religious free exercise rights, and probably of freedom of speech and association as well. In other words, the problem is theological, not constitutional; it reflects a tension in religious self-understanding.

The First Amendment's Establishment Clause and Free Exercise Clause protect religious freedom: "Congress shall make no law respecting an establishment of religion, or prohibiting the free exercise thereof." The first prohibits the establishment of an official or state church. The second protects our individual freedom of conscience and belief as well as our collective ability to choose forms of worship, ecclesial organization, and other matters of religious practice, including prophetic practice. While there is some tension between the two clauses, they generally work together to protect religious freedom by preventing government coercion or interference in matters of conscience and faith. Historically, this pattern marked a significant break with the models of church-state relations that had been common in Europe and throughout the world. By keeping state and religious institutions independent of each other, the American founders simultaneously freed religion from state control and freed the state from religious control. The American system, says church-state scholar James Wood, "denies government the right to use religion for the accomplishment of political ends and denies religion the right to use government for the accomplishment of religious ends."[131]

The U.S. Supreme Court has unequivocally affirmed the right of religious people and institutions to be involved in public life and to advocate religiously grounded positions on public and political issues. The First Amendment, in other words, is not a barrier to prophetic activity. In *Walz v. Tax Commission*, decided in 1970, the Court noted:

> Adherents of particular faiths and individual churches frequently take strong positions on public issues including . . . vigorous advocacy of legal or constitutional positions. Of course, churches as much as secular bodies and private citizens have that right.[132]

Eight years later, in *McDaniel v. Paty*, the Court unanimously invalidated a Tennessee law that prohibited clergy from serving in the state legislature. In his concurring opinion, Justice William J. Brennan Jr. commented on public religious activity and its relation to the First Amendment:

> The mere fact that a purpose of the Establishment Clause is to reduce or eliminate religious divisiveness or strife, does not place religious discussion, association, or political participation in a status less preferred than rights of discussion, association, and political participation generally. . . .

> Government may not as a goal promote "safe thinking" with respect to religion and fence out from political participation those, such as ministers, whom it regards as overinvolved in religion. Religionists no less than members of any other group enjoy the full measure of protection afforded speech, association, and political activity generally. The Establishment Clause, properly understood, is a shield against any attempt by government to

inhibit religion as it has done here. It may not be used as a sword to justify repression of religion or its adherents from any aspect of public life.[133]

In other words, religious independence from the state does not preclude prophetic engagement with the society. Prophetic practice, like other forms of religious exercise, is consistent with the Establishment Clause and protected by the First Amendment. Thus, liberal reluctance to engage in public religious expression based on First Amendment concerns is misplaced.

To say that liberal prophetic practice is protected by the First Amendment is not the end of the story. Some may object that, although this practice is legal, we should refrain lest we unwittingly contribute to the already weakening church-state separation. However, true prophetic practice that speaks from the depth of theological tradition and refuses to identify itself with a particular political authority has a positive impact on religious freedom. It simultaneously depends on and supports the democratic traditions of freedom of dissent and church-state separation. By fulfilling its justice-seeking role, prophetic activity helps preserve the social and political space on which these traditions depend. In other words, public prophetic religion, including liberal prophetic practice at its best, strengthens rather than undermines separation of church and state.

We can see this at work in the biblical prophets, whose practices form the deepest roots of our own prophetic social justice work. In the early Israelite society from which the prophetic tradition emerged, there was no distinction between religion and politics, much less any separation of church and state. But as the practice of prophetic critique became institutionalized, a form of separation of powers protecting it developed as well. To understand this process, we must examine the role the prophets played within their own societies. At the most basic level, they functioned as intermediaries between the divine and human worlds. In the Deuteronomic passage relating to prophets, God says, "I will put my words in the mouth of the prophet, who shall speak to [the people] everything that I command."[134] They are God's spokespersons, and their pronouncements are understood as divine messages that almost always are related to situations of injustice, especially those involving oppression or exploitation of the weakest members of society. When the prophets denounce injustice, they are announcing God's judgment.[135]

At one time, people commonly thought of prophets as charismatic loners who lived in isolation and spoke as social outsiders.[136] Today, however, biblical scholars accept that the prophets were fully part of their own societies, although they were often critical of the practices they witnessed.[137] But they did not all occupy the same social positions. Scholars commonly distinguish between two basic types of prophets: central prophets, who belonged to the socially empowered establishment, and peripheral prophets, who belonged to socially marginalized or devalued groups.[138] This distinction is not sharp; the prophets' roles varied as societies changed, and some prophets seem to have occupied different social locations during their careers.[139] Moreover, the very nature of the prophetic role may have moderated these distinctions. Even the most socially marginalized prophets were empowered by their mission as God's spokespersons, just as the most privileged were often critical of others of their own social rank. Nevertheless, the differences in the prophets' social status and power affected the nature of their prophetic pronouncements.

Biblical scholar Robert Wilson points out the importance of social networks for peripheral prophets who did not have the institutional support that central prophets received from their association with other social and political leaders. Peripheral prophets' support groups may have been small and perhaps socially marginalized, but these prophets were important agents of social change because they spoke not only on behalf of God, but also on behalf of the marginalized groups they represented. Then as now, socially marginalized groups sought increased power and pressed for radical social restructuring. The prophets served as vehicles for communicating the groups' needs and goals to the larger society. The prophets' status as divine intermediaries meant that the interests of the groups they represented were in some sense identified with God's interests, so the larger society often agreed to some of the desired changes.[140]

Central prophets were normally more conservative than peripheral prophets. They typically held official positions within the social and political establishment, often acting as advisors to the king. One of their important functions was to help maintain social stability. For this reason, they were likely to resist outside demands for radical innovation, instead preferring gradual social change. While these prophets sometimes pronounced critical judgments on society and the king, they were, according to Wilson, "likely to do so under the guise of retaining or restoring traditional beliefs and attitudes."[141]

We normally think of calls to restore traditional values as the opposite of progressive social change. But it would be a mistake to equate the affirmation of traditional values with conservative resistance to social change. In Israelite society during the eighth century BCE monarchy, for example, power and wealth had become highly concentrated, leaving the majority of the population strained and destitute—much like American society at the beginning of the twentieth-first century.[142] The problem, as the prophets understood it, was that society had fallen away from the more egalitarian values of the covenant. The great eighth century prophets were highly critical of these developments, especially their impact on the poor. Isaiah of Jerusalem, for example, denounces judges who take bribes and fail to give proper justice in cases involving "the orphan and the widow."[143] Amos calls divine judgment on those who "sell the righteous for silver, and the needy for a pair of sandals," a reference to the practice of debt slavery, and on creditors who prostrate themselves in worship "on garments taken in pledge"—a violation of covenant laws relating to money lending.[144] Biblical scholar D. N. Premnath notes that

> one thing we learn from the prophets is that poverty or injustice is no accident. They knew exactly what the causes were and who was responsible for it. They did not speak in abstraction. They knew what the oppression/injustice was, and who the oppressors and oppressed were.[145]

In this situation, a call to return to traditional covenantal norms of justice—including periodically freeing debt slaves, wealth redistribution, and restricting other practices of wealthy owners and creditors—is a radical move.[146]

The political and moral independence of the peripheral prophets is to a degree inherent in their social location. But the Deuteronomic laws specifying leadership roles also created a structural independence, even for central prophets. Here we can see a clear division of authority or separation of powers. Justice was to be administered by judges, and in certain instances, by Levitical priests. The people were allowed to choose a king, but unlike the situation in many early societies, the king was neither deified nor placed above the law. Moreover, the king's power was limited by laws prohibiting him from exercising priestly functions.[147]

The Deuteronomic laws also specified the role of the prophets. The people were instructed not to turn to the intermediaries used by other nations; they were to rely on Mosaic prophets whom God would raise up from among the people.[148] Significantly, this role was to be exclusive and independent of the king's authority. Prophetic judgments against kingly wrongdoing served in part to remind the king that his authority was subordinate to God's.[149] Breaches of these boundaries did not go unnoticed by the prophets. Samuel condemned Saul for usurping priestly functions,[150] and Nathan rebuked David for abusing his power by sending Uriah to his death so he could marry Bathsheba.[151]

By carrying out their primary roles as intermediaries between God and the people, often bringing God's critical judgments to bear on unjust social realities, the prophets sought to preserve the proper covenantal relationship between God and the people. Their critical judgments were grounded in covenantal norms that were independent of the programs of particular kings and to which the kings knew themselves to be bound. As a result, even when they were highly critical, the prophets were understood as performing essential social and moral roles within the community. By the very act of fulfilling their divine call, the prophets carved out and protected the social and political space their role required.

Finally, by providing for judges, kings, priests, and prophets, and by assigning each group a set of specific and exclusive functions, the Deuteronomic law created the structural space, what we might call the constitutional framework, for a separation of powers. Through this separation of powers and the prophetic critique it enabled, the practice of religiously grounded social and political dissent was institutionalized. Unitarian Universalist theologian James Luther Adams summarizes:

> Old Testament prophetism institutionalized dissent and criticism and thus initiated the separation of powers. The prophets said that the culture was not under the control of centralized power; viable culture requires the institutionalization of dissent— in other words, the freedom to criticize the powers that be.[152]

Both ancient Israelite society and modern democracies impose limits on the power of rulers by locating ultimate authority in sources that lie beyond their control. In biblical society, the true source of political authority was God, and the moral duties of leaders were expressed in the norms of the covenant. In liberal democracies, the ultimate source of political power is said to rest in the people, and leaders are expected to follow the moral and political principles embodied in the Constitution and in other universally accepted norms, such as international human rights principles. But these limits on authority, however deeply engrained in principle and tradition, need institutional structures to make them effective amid the contingencies of political challenges and the economic and social pressures of daily life. The ancient Israelites accomplished this by the division of leadership functions discussed above. The role of the prophets was especially important in maintaining this separation of powers because their judgments held all leaders accountable to the norms of the covenant.

Modern democracies continue the practices of separation of powers and official accountability based on higher principles with structural restraints on state power. These structures include the checks and balances created by separating governmental functions into independent legislative, executive, and judicial branches, and by the federal system that allocates power among local and central authorities. Restraints may also be created through such practices as limitations on terms of office or periodic elections. In theory, the ultimate limit on state power resides in the right of the people to choose new leaders.

Modern democratic societies no longer create official institutional roles for prophets or other critics of those in political power. But the First Amendment's protections institutionalize the deeply engrained custom of political dissent and criticism of the government. The Supreme Court has said that public officials must expect criticism as a consequence of their public office.[153] Criticism comes from many sources, perhaps most visibly by opposing political parties or persons who have economic or other self-interested motives for urging political change. Religiously grounded prophetic critique is another source of criticism, one that is especially important because of its independence and grounding in moral norms relating to justice. From this perspective, prophetic practice is as much an expression of dissent as an exercise of religion. Moreover, by highlighting the injustices that affect society's most vulnerable and excluded members, the prophets broaden the democratic polity by insisting on including more of its members and expanding the range of voices heard in the public square. The constitutional protection afforded prophetic critique might be seen as a way of institutionalizing this important practice.

This is not to say that the liberal fear of too close a connection between religion and politics is unfounded. Establishment concerns are raised when religious agendas become, or threaten to become, public policy or when government officials justify their official actions on religious grounds. We see this in the increasingly overlapping identities of the religious and political right. When religious groups are too closely identified with the state, or when they have unfettered access to the channels of economic and political power, they can easily become theological apologists for unjust government policies and social conditions. This status makes true prophetic practice impossible. Worse, a serious threat to religious freedom exists when public officials and political candidates implicitly and sometimes explicitly endorse the positions of particular religious groups. Some of the religious right's public proclamations are a form of theological bullying, a practice hardly consistent with First Amendment values.

A similar danger arises when religious or political leaders speak of America as a Christian nation. When people use this phrase, they do not simply point to the historical influence of Christian ideals; they claim that Christianity should somehow become normative. They may press for things like posting the Ten Commandments in public buildings and prayer in public schools. Many believe that their own religious freedom is violated without such measures. They believe, in other words, that the state should actively promote religion, or at least their particular form of Christianity. Supporting government-sponsored religious practices in the name of religious freedom constitutes a serious disconnect. Our religious freedom is weakened, not strengthened, by official support of religious activities. Those who want the government to sanction their religious practices seek religious power, not religious freedom.

Liberal prophetic practice is rooted in the tradition of the biblical prophets and sustained by the long-standing liberal religious commitment to social justice. Its passion, vision, and sources of inspiration lie in these religious traditions, not in any form of state sponsorship or control. Prophetic religion, if true to its heritage, can never become a tool of the state. Indeed, the state is often the target of liberal prophetic practice, and religious liberalism's independence from the state makes effective prophetic critique possible. Under these circumstances, there is no danger of creating an unhealthy establishment or quasi-establishment of religion. A society that recognizes the vital role of the prophetic voice, a society that creates the legal and social space for it to be heard even when it makes us uncomfortable will be a healthier and more just society. And a religious tradition that values freedom can help preserve the social space for this critical prophetic voice.

Liberal Religion, Democracy
and Empire

WE FACE A CRITICAL moment in the life of our democracy. The crisis arises out of a particular tension in the American identity—handed down by our European forebears—and pulls simultaneously toward democracy and empire. The United States has periodically struggled to preserve its democratic spirit in the face of its own imperial impulses. Our European forebears seem to have had a disposition for both freedom and conquest. In philosopher Cornel West's words, "The contingent origins of American democracy and the ignoble beginnings of imperial America go hand in hand."[154]

In recent years, the American impulse toward empire has been on the rise. Scholars note that imperial policies accelerated sharply following the end of the Cold War in 1989 and have become increasingly dominant since 9/11.[155] Observers from across the political spectrum have remarked that this flexing of American imperial muscle has come at the expense of American democracy. Historian Andrew Bacevich, a Republican and retired career military officer, claims that "American democracy in our time has suffered notable decay,"[156] and that the American proclivity for global power projection threatens "the destruction of what most Americans profess to hold dear."[157] West, a liberal scholar, points to "a deeply troubling deterioration of democratic powers in America today."[158]

Urgent challenges confront us. As religious liberals who support democratic values and cooperative uses of power, how can we help nurture the weakened democratic spirit and push back against the forces of empire? What theological and spiritual resources can we bring to this struggle, and how can we most effectively use them? In short, how do we engage in liberal prophetic practice under a condition of empire?

The Impulse Toward Empire

American empire is not just a matter of global dominance but involves a combination of both external and internal projections of power.[159] External power projection consists primarily of U.S. military presence, global economic power, and the worldwide influence of American culture. Internal power projection involves increasing concentrations of economic and political power in the hands of fewer and fewer people as well as the blending of governmental and corporate power that gives large corporations unparalleled influence over public policy. These internal power projections are most responsible for the undermining of our democracy. Yet the internal and external dimensions of American empire are parts of a larger whole, and both shape the context within which liberal prophetic voices must speak.

The American empire of the twenty-first century differs from empires of both the distant and the recent past, such as ancient Rome or Nazi Germany. Rather than conquer other societies in order to rule them directly, the U.S. practice relies on indirect influence through various forms of pressure and intervention.[160] By the same token, internal control is maintained not by suppressing political opposition or applying police state tactics, but by manipulating existing political and legal structures in ways that appear to support them but in fact distort or subvert them. Political philosopher Sheldon Wolin uses the phrase "inverted totalitarianism" to describe this system. He does not mean that the U.S. government is totalitarian in the traditional sense, like Nazi Germany or the former Soviet Union. Rather, American imperial power exerts itself in certain totalizing tendencies toward control, expansion, and dominance.[161]

The American impulse toward empire is rooted in the ideologies of militarism and capitalism that, like all ideologies, are grounded in a specific worldview and reflect a set of core values. West calls them "aggressive militarism" and "free-market fundamentalism" and sees them as "dominating, antidemocratic dogmas."[162] We can better understand how these dogmas work in the service of empire if we look at them not simply as social or political ideologies but as theologies.

Theology of Violence

The dogma of aggressive militarism is part of a deeper theology of violence. In the American context, it points to a disposition to use violence, and especially the military, to accomplish national goals. Bacevich refers to this condition as the "new militarism."[163] Both religious and political liberals must understand that the dogma of military aggression was part of the American theology long before the Bush administration's bellicose response to 9/11. American militarism goes back at least to World War I, and its deep roots lie in the period of European colonial conquest and the glorification of violence that has always been part of our culture. Moreover, this dogma is not simply the domain of political conservatives. Bacevich notes that during the 2008 presidential election campaign, no candidate in either party questioned either the logic or the wisdom of the policy of global military dominance.[164] In the first weeks of his presidency, President Barack Obama affirmed a commitment to "maintain our military dominance [and] have the strongest armed forces in the history of the world."[165] Certainly the overall approach of President Obama's foreign policy favors international cooperation rather than the gunslinger unilateralism of his predecessor, but militarism remains entrenched in America's identity.

Maintaining a global military force of more than seven hundred bases in over one hundred countries is not cheap. If the way we spend our money reflects our values, then militarism is indeed a deeply held value. The United States spends more today on the military than at any time in its history, both in real dollars adjusted for inflation and as a percentage of the federal budget. By some calculations, we spend more on defense than all other nations in the world combined.[166] The upshot is that we have the strongest military machine the world has ever seen; no other nation or bloc of nations even comes close. But our military might has become divorced from its nominal purpose, national defense. No one seriously argues that we need this much military power for actual defense against credible threats.[167] Our militaristic worldview has become normalized and is taken for granted, while preparing for and actually waging war "has become [our] normal state and seemingly permanent condition."[168]

Most theologies include what theologians call a *soteriology*, a doctrine about salvation or deliverance. The theology of violence is no different. In this theology, violence itself brings us salvation. Theologian Walter Wink calls this "the myth of redemptive violence."[169] Like religious mythologies everywhere, its story is ritualistically told and retold so that its explanatory power is continually reinforced.

The basic story line is always the same. Think of any western movie or any modern equivalent such as *Star Wars*, any police or detective story, any superhero story. In every case, "bad" violence, symbolizing the evil we must conquer, is overcome by "good" violence. The good guys bring the bad guys to justice by applying superior force, and sometimes superior intelligence, either by capturing or killing them. This mythological narrative is repeated in children's cartoons and video games, many of which are cast in explicitly militaristic terms. Our children learn the salvific power of force and violence at an early age. This deeply engrained worldview seems perfectly normal. "Violence is so successful as a myth precisely because it does not seem to be mythic in the least," Wink declares. "Violence simply appears to be the nature of things."[170]

In political contexts, the military becomes the divinely chosen instrument of our salvation. The theology of violence thus gives divine sanction to military power used in the service of national/imperial policies. War is deeply embedded in our national narrative—in the stories we tell about ourselves as a people. Stories of war have always been part of the American story, and as these stories are told and retold over time, they become self-legitimizing. Theologian Stanley Hauerwas argues that "war continues to seem necessary because we have found no way to tell the stories of our lives in which war does not play a role."[171] And Bacevich notes that as the state of war is perceived as normal rather than as an exception to the normal state of peace, our global military supremacy has "come to signify who we are and what we stand for."[172] In other words, in the theology of violence, war is not just about what we do, it is about *who we are.*

79

Theology of Free-Market Fundamentalism

The second antidemocratic dogma, free-market fundamentalism, is an ideology that supports the accumulation of unlimited
wealth and power in the hands of global corporations, and justi-
fies the obscene level of wealth inequality in the United States.
As with militarism, we may think of free-market fundamentalism
not simply as a political or economic ideology but as a theology.
In free-market theology, the market becomes the god whose
divinely ordained processes create order and balance in the universe. Theologian Harvey Cox points out that, like other gods,
the market-god is looked upon by its worshippers with mystery
and reverence, and endowed with a range of divine attributes that
"are not always completely evident to mortals but must be trusted
and affirmed by faith."[73] Here too we have a doctrine of salvation. In free-market theology, the market itself is the god that
will bring us salvation, as long as we don't disturb its natural order
through regulation. Moreover, the divinely chosen instrument
for this purpose is the multinational corporation. Corporate power
itself therefore takes on certain divine attributes. Like most gods,
its authority becomes self-justifying, and it therefore has no need
for moral accountability. The economic meltdown that began
with the collapse of our financial system in 2008 has shown—
if we needed to be shown—that this false god cannot save us. Yet
the bailout of large and often corrupt financial institutions and
the extreme reluctance to impose even the most basic regulatory
reform suggest that faith in this god continues unabated.[74]

The theology of conservative Christian evangelicalism has
long been used to justify this market ideology. Economic historian Gordon Bigelow notes the connections between the early
evangelical view of original sin, in which poverty was seen as part

of the divine plan for redemption through suffering, and the social misery produced by nineteenth-century Western industrial capitalism. This theological perspective justified the wealth accumulated by the capitalist class as part of the divine plan.[175] The Christian right today continues to support economic policies that favor the accumulation of private wealth. Beginning in 2005, for example, Focus on the Family and other conservative evangelical organizations recast the federal estate tax—which affects only the wealthiest Americans—as a tax on the family. They joined with conservative Republican leaders to pass legislation significantly reducing the amount of wealth subject to the tax, increasing the exemption from $1.5 million in 2005 to $5 million in 2011.[176]

Defenders of free-market fundamentalism continue to trust in the market as though it were a utopian vision embedded in a higher order of natural law. Bigelow describes the vision as an "imagined place, where equilibrium rules, consumers get what they want, and the fairest outcomes occur as if the neoclassical theory of the free market were incontrovertible, endorsed by science and ordained by God."[177]

Yet this theological vision is unsustainable. Dutch philosopher Hans Achterhuis persuasively argues that free-market capitalism should be understood precisely as a form of utopia. Like all utopias, he argues, the free market cannot live up to its own idealized claims and ultimately moves toward its opposite, dystopia.[178] The current worldwide economic crisis was largely brought about by an excessive faith in this utopian ideal.

Since the end of the Cold War and the Reagan administration's aggressive deregulation of American business—a policy largely continued by the Clinton administration—free-market fundamentalism has increasingly become the guiding theology of government policy as well as corporate practice. The result is a unique and dangerous blending of corporate and state power. Corporate relationship to the state shifted from seeking to influence government policy and legislation to what Wolin calls "managed democracy." In this system, the state increasingly relies on corporate economic power to advance its policies. The result is "a symbiotic relationship between traditional government and the system of 'private' governance represented by the modern business corporation,"[179] culminating in the "ultimate merger . . . between capitalism and democracy."[180]

Consequences of Empire

The union of globalized corporations and the government has dangerous and far-reaching consequences. It is fundamentally antidemocratic, because the corporations that share this enormous power are neither answerable to the electorate nor subject to the limits on state power imposed by the Constitution. American empire has its own unwritten constitution, one that sanctions vast public and private powers limited only by opportunity and ambition. Wolin's stark conclusion is that the imperial tendencies expressed through militarism, globalized capital, and the alliance of corporate and state power undermine one of the most basic principles of the American political system, that "the Constitution provides the standard for a government of limited powers, and that American governance and politics are democratic."[181] He argues that American democracy cannot be revitalized until the American people and their political leaders squarely confront this reality.

Beyond structural issues, the fundamentalist theologies of empire also undermine what we might call the spiritual dimensions of democracy by diminishing our understanding of citizenship. Bacevich has observed that empire requires a "minimalist" concept of citizenship.[182] While it expects loyalty and patriotism, it resists a truly engaged citizenry, one that asks too many hard questions or challenges entrenched power structures. Empire prefers its citizens to be subjects rather than agents, demobilized and passive rather than organized and active. It encourages this disengagement by fostering what Wolin calls "an atmosphere of collective fear and of individual powerlessness."[183] The fear may be directed toward specific possibilities such as terrorist attacks, losing one's job or health insurance, or not having enough money in retirement, but the object of the fear is unimportant. The goal is to maintain a generalized feeling of insecurity and powerlessness. When citizens live in a constant state of anxiety, and when they feel powerless to change the circumstances that create their anxiety, they are more likely to withdraw, seeking to protect what they have rather than to mobilize for change. In a sense, the people are simply worn down or "hammered into resignation."[184]

Other systemic factors impinge on democratic citizenship. Discussion of important public issues takes place at a remarkably shallow level. Political candidates as well as the public are often uninformed or misinformed, and political events such as debates or town meetings are highly scripted and almost willfully uninformative. Strident and highly partisan talk shows only make things worse. The dumbed-down nature of our public discourse makes serious engagement with important issues nearly impossible and undermines our democracy. As this condition becomes the normal operating mode, people lose faith in the prospects for public discourse altogether.[185]

The endless opinion polls thrust at us by the media and their corporate owners further distance us from the political process.

These polls create the illusion of meaningful participation by inviting citizens to express their views on current issues and candidates, but they are typically structured so that only shallow and meaningless responses are permitted (yes/no; agree/disagree; don't know). They leave no room for ambiguity or nuance. Worse, polls involve a low-risk, no-cost form of pseudo-involvement. Responding to a poll entails no follow-up political responsibility or commitment.

Polls are then given the appearance of meaning as pollsters and pundits parse the data, sagely reporting the views and trends among subgroups such as white males over forty, Hispanic voters under thirty, female college graduates, and so on. But this information is useful not to voters but to candidates, who use it to target different segments of the electorate with messages designed to appeal to their preferences or prejudices. By highlighting the places of division and disagreement, this process can lead to mistrust among voters and make organizing around common interests difficult.[186]

The right to vote is commonly understood as the ultimate democratic practice, bringing the power back to the people. Certainly voting is an important citizen responsibility, one to be taken seriously, and includes the responsibility to be fully informed about the issues and the candidates' qualifications and experience. Yet voter turnout in American elections is abysmally low. In addition, being fully, or even adequately informed, is next to impossible—and this is not simply the result of voter laziness or disinterest. Structural features in our system contribute to this state of affairs.

One factor in low voter participation is the widespread, justifiable feeling of powerlessness, the sense that voting doesn't really change anything. Our highly managed political and electoral system produces candidates who represent the interests of the existing imperial structures rather than the needs of ordinary citizens. It's not that candidates and public officials all think alike; indeed, deep ideological divisions contribute to the government gridlock we have witnessed in recent years. But despite these philosophical differences, the structural inertia of empire ensures that switching a few faces in Congress or even changing the ruling party is not likely to alter the dominant imperial structures or produce any real change in government practices. The persuasive power of the citizen's vote is no match for the persuasive power of the corporate purse. Washington lobbyists and their corporate employers remind us of who and what our representatives really represent.

Worse, despite the public spectacle of political campaigns, the forces of empire actively discourage voting. The bizarrely ironic message that voters should not trust the government, incessantly pushed by many candidates and elected officials, encourages alienation and tells voters not to bother seeking help from those elected to serve them. An even more cynical tactic is the recent proliferation of state laws that ostensibly protect against voter fraud, but whose barely disguised purpose is to restrict voter eligibility. These laws employ a range of techniques, such as strict photo identification requirements, reduced opportunities for early voting, and restrictions on voter registration drives. A recent independent study concludes that these laws will make voting more difficult for over five million people, primarily "young, minority, and low-income voters, as well as voters with disabilities"—in other words, those most likely to vote against entrenched power interests.[187] A more blatantly antidemocratic set of laws is hard to imagine but for the example of the poll taxes, bogus literacy tests, and other such tactics finally overthrown by the passage of the

1965 Voting Rights Act. Making this connection explicit, U.S. Attorney General Eric Holder announced, in December 2011 that the Justice Department was investigating these new laws using its authority under this Act.[188]

Revitalizing Democracy

In the face of these realities, let us consider the prospects for liberal prophetic practice. We can start by remembering that the American impulse toward empire is only one side of the coin. The impulse toward democracy still beats in the American breast. In fact, despite his harsh assessment of our current situation, Cornell West believes that the forces of democracy are ultimately the stronger of the two. He maintains that "the voices and views of nihilistic imperialism may currently dominate our discourse, but they are not the authentic voice of American democracy."[189] Wolin believes that the days of American global economic dominance are over,[190] and Bacevich argues that the current policies of global military power projection and perpetual war are unsustainable and beginning to collapse under their own weight.[191] Each of these prominent figures sees that current circumstances create openings through which a revitalized democracy may begin to emerge. But this impulse toward democracy is not self-perpetuating. Our liberal prophetic actions, working in concert with other concerned individuals and groups, must keep it alive and healthy.

This work will not be easy. We cannot start from scratch; "it is not morning in America," says Wolin.[192] Whatever opportunities for renewal are available at this moment in our history, they bear the weight of current imperial structures, and although the forces of empire may be waning, they are not likely to disappear. A globalized economy is here to stay, and constantly shifting global power structures involving the interplay of governmental and private actors are a part of the twenty-first century. Our challenge is to nurture a prophetic counterweight to check these impulses toward expansion and domination and help create breathing space for democracy.

We must draw on the core values and commitments shared by democracy and religious liberalism as we seek to direct our prophetic practice toward this vital task. At the same time, we must remember that liberal democracy as a political tradition and liberal religion as a faith tradition are not interchangeable. We must also be aware that, as religious liberals, we are not immune to the internal tensions that can weaken our voices and the external forces of empire that constantly play on us.

Points of commonality between democracy and religious liberalism include their mutual commitments to moral and religious pluralism, non-coercive human relationships, fair and open process, and a fundamental orientation toward justice. The deep core of both traditions, however, is their mutual commitment to freedom and equality. These shared core values, as well as the points of disagreement, can help shape our prophetic practice to defend democracy against the forces of empire.[193]

Religious liberalism's understanding of human freedom is grounded in its affirmation of the inherent worth and dignity of all persons, which is rooted in the biblical concept of *imago Dei* — the belief that we are all created in God's image (although some religious liberals prefer non-biblical language). This affirmation is in part a claim about the nature of our existence as human beings, or what theologians call *theological anthropology*. It is also a moral claim that each of us, by virtue of being human, is entitled to be treated with dignity and respect. This affirmation therefore has both individual and social implications. Our inherent worth and dignity means that all human beings have a right to a meaningful and fulfilling life, and this requires communities based on justice, respect, and mutuality. For religious liberals, then, human liberation is the end toward which our freedom is to be directed. Liberal theologians often speak of this goal in terms of human flourishing or human fulfillment.[194] This liberation is part of the vision that helps guide liberal prophetic practice.

This understanding of human freedom necessarily includes a commitment to human equality: The inherent worth and dignity of persons means the *equal* worth and dignity of *all* persons. The concept of equal worth is both an anthropological claim about the nature of our humanness and an ethical claim about the kinds of social relationships we require. Because we are of equal worth, each of us has an inherent and irreducible value as well as a right to a meaningful and fulfilling life. Our equal worth also implies a moral obligation to create the conditions within which human fulfillment can be fully realized. Religious liberalism recognizes that human flourishing and fulfillment—human liberation—can be realized only in a context of justice in which social oppressions are overcome. This commitment is the foundation of the liberal emphasis on creating just institutions, including just political structures, that enable all persons to live with dignity and respect. In the liberal commitment to human freedom, personal liberation and social liberation are inextricably linked, and both contribute to the vision that orients liberal prophetic practice.

Freedom and equality are also among the defining principles of democracy. Political philosopher Michael Perry frames these principles in language remarkably similar to that used by religious liberals: "The foundational moral commitment of liberal democracy is to the true and full humanity of *every* person — and, therefore, to the inviolability of *every* person."[195] However, there are some differences in the way the two traditions understand this freedom. In religious liberalism, freedom is understood primarily as an attribute of the person. Human freedom has social and political implications because it demands social arrangements and institutional structures that best enable its full expression, but its primary locus is the person.

In the liberal political theory that underlies democracy, in contrast, freedom specifies the relationship between the individual and the state. Most contemporary political philosophers do not bother to work out elaborate conceptions of what it means to be human, what we might think of as a philosophical counterpart to a theological anthropology. Human freedom is real but serves mainly as the justification for guaranteeing particular liberties such as freedom of speech and religion against infringement by the state. We might say that in a democracy, freedom is something we *have*, while in religious liberalism, it is part of who we *are*. Yet for both traditions, freedom is best preserved in structures of human relationships and forms of political organization that best enable human beings to develop and flourish. Democracy is, or should be, one of these forms. Ideally, democracy "is about the conditions that make it possible for ordinary people to better their lives," says Wolin, "by becoming political beings and by making power responsive to their hopes and needs."[196]

Equality is also one of the core values of democracy. Political philosophers disagree about the nature of equality and its relationship to freedom, but we can overlook these philosophical fine points. Philosopher Ronald Dworkin's views are worth noting, however, because his understanding of equality most resembles that of religious liberalism. Equality is about treating persons with "equal concern and respect."[197] As a political concept, in a democracy, the government should show equal concern for all citizens:

> No government is legitimate that does not show equal concern
> for the fate of all those citizens over whom it claims dominion
> and from whom it claims allegiance. Equal concern is the sovereign virtue of political community—without it government is
> only tyranny.[198]

As with other political theorists, Dworkin's claim does not rest on a deeper claim about the nature of persons. In other words, it is a political, not a theological, affirmation. But for religious liberals, the inherent worth and dignity of persons is a theological claim. This distinction suggests that our prophetic challenge to empire might be strengthened by combining the liberal theological principle with Dworkin's equality principle. Our prophetic message claims that a democratic government should treat us with equal concern not only because of its obligation to its citizens, but also because the nature of our humanness demands it. This idea has practical implications. Dworkin argues that a government's obligation to show equal concern for all comes into question when the nation's wealth is distributed highly unequally, as it is in the United States. Prophetic action demanding change in our economic structures is thus supported by deeply rooted principles of both liberal theology and liberal democracy.

The shared commitment to freedom and equality means that religious liberalism can be an important ally in the struggle against empire simply by acting on our own deepest values. Yet simply affirming a set of compatible concepts is not enough. These ideas must be transformed from abstraction into action. They must be infused with a spiritual vitality that can sustain our struggle over the long haul.

West identifies three basic commitments within our democratic tradition. They are deeply engrained in the American psyche and form part of what Wolin calls the "culture of democracy," a "complex of beliefs, values, and practices that nurture equality, cooperation, and freedom" and support democratic practices.[199] West calls these basic democratic commitments the "Socratic commitment to questioning," the "prophetic commitment to justice," and the "tragicomic commitment to hope." These commitments are the spiritual wellsprings of a reinvigorated democracy and they are also basic to religious liberalism. Drawing on them in our prophetic practice will deepen our faith even as we nurture the culture of democracy and contribute to the struggle against empire.

West traces the democratic tradition of questioning to Socrates. Anyone who has been to law school will recognize the technique. But here West means not clever verbal sparring, but a commitment to truth-seeking and truth-speaking, requiring "a relentless self-examination and critique of institutions of authority, motivated by an endless quest for intellectual integrity and moral consistency."[200] This commitment draws on the democratic preference for forms of public discussion that involve reason-giving. True democratic dialogue is not simply about expressing our opinions and preferences; it requires that we justify our positions.

A commitment to questioning, and especially to self-examination and the critique of authority, has always been part of the liberal religious tradition. It emerged from the Enlightenment principles of personal autonomy and free critical inquiry. In practice, all claims of external authority, whether from government, denominational institutions, or ministers and congregational leaders, are subject to challenge. Perhaps we can have more patience with the incessant questioning and endless debate at denominational gatherings—indeed, constant questioning seems to be a form of liberal spiritual practice—if we understand it as part of the long tradition that informs both democracy and religious liberalism.

West's reminder to call leaders and institutions of authority to account does not preclude engaging in self-examination with equal intellectual honesty. Unitarian Universalist ethicist Sharon Welch notes that "the premise of liberalism can best be served by honestly examining the barriers to social transformation found within the liberal tradition."[201] As we struggle against the injustices of empire, we must also reflect honestly and critically on how we have contributed to or acquiesced in these conditions. The practice of self-critique forms an important part of liberal religious self-understanding and enables us to contribute to revitalizing our democracy just by doing what we have always done best.

West's second element, the prophetic commitment to justice, can be traced to the prophets of the Hebrew Bible. Like prophets in all ages, they spoke out against injustice and called their leaders to account. Prophetic witness, says West,

> consists of human acts of justice and kindness that attend to the unjust sources of human hurt and misery. Prophetic witness calls attention to the causes of unjustified suffering and unnecessary social misery. It highlights personal and institutional evil, including especially the evil of being indifferent to personal and institutional evil.[202]

The prophetic commitment to justice builds on critical Socratic questioning and calls our communities to spiritual and social transformation. The prophetic voice speaks not only on behalf of the poor and the oppressed but also against those who misuse power. Here too the liberal religious tradition has made

an important contribution. Liberal religion has always empha-
sized ethics over doctrine, and religious liberals have always been
among those who call society to account in the face of injustice,
challenge the cultural status quo, and work for the dismantling
of unjust institutions and the creation of just ones.

West's third element is what he calls a "tragicomic commitment to hope." This is not simply about being optimistic, but
involves a deeper form of spirituality: the ability to persevere, to
continue the struggle for justice even when all seems hopeless.
He describes this kind of hope as "the ability to laugh and retain
a sense of life's joy—to preserve hope even while staring in the
face of hate and hypocrisy—as against falling into the nihilism of
paralyzing despair."[203]

Welch astutely examines liberal middle-class activists' tendency
toward despair when seeking quick or definitive solutions to social
problems. But such solutions are never possible, and measuring
the success of justice work against unattainable goals drains prophetic energy. Our desire for control can also lead to frustration
and resignation. We want to respond to injustice, but in our own
way, on our own terms. Welch suggests that this need for control
leads to discouragement when things don't go as planned. The
result is that religious liberals often have trouble sustaining their
motivation to work for change over the long term.[204]

But a long-term view is essential if our prophetic practice is to
be effective. We must be willing to participate in the struggle for
justice against the forces of empire even if we can't define all the
terms of our involvement, and even when we can't control the
outcome. Welch suggests that we should measure our involvement "as much by the possibilities it creates as by its immediate
results."[205] In other words, responsible prophetic practice means
changing what we can in the present while also creating the

"conditions of possibility" for further changes by others.[206] Hope comes from acknowledging that the struggle for justice is always long-term and from knowing that our tentative and often halting small steps form an important part of this larger process.

Hope has always played a central role in the liberal religious tradition. In the early nineteenth century, Universalists offered a doctrinal basis for human hope. Their belief in universal salvation stood in stark contrast to the Calvinist doctrine of election that condemned most of humanity to the hopelessness of eternal damnation. On the social level, liberals have always had deep faith in the possibilities of human fulfillment and social progress. But West's notion of tragicomic hope is a bit different, a gentle critique of the liberal tendency to be overly optimistic or to swing the other way and lapse into despair. He reminds us that

> this kind of tragicomic hope is dangerous—and potentially subversive—because it can never be extinguished. Like laughter, dance, and music, it is a form of elemental freedom that cannot be eliminated or snuffed out by any elite power.[207]

For this reason, it is one of our key resources in the struggle against empire.

Ethicist Jeffrey Stout links this kind of hope to democracy. Democratic hope, he says,

> is the hope of making a difference for the better by democratic means. The question of hope is whether a difference can be made, not whether progress is being made or whether human beings will work it all out in the end. . . . I take for granted that our condition is always bad enough in some respects to disturb anybody with a conscience. . . . I also take for granted . . . that there are grounds for hope and humor if we look hard enough in the right places.[208]

The tension between democracy and empire seems to be a permanent feature of the American condition. By the same token, religious liberals seem cursed to live with the tension between energizing hope and the temptation toward paralyzing cynicism. But we must recognize that cynicism is a luxury of privilege, a negative spirituality that in the end only feeds the forces of empire. We can maintain our hope, and be true to our own religious ideals, if we remember that this very dissonance, this tension that so often frustrates us, can be creative as well as destructive. It can fuel the passion to question, the courage to be prophetic, and the faith to hope.

Epilogue:
Liberal Religious Identity

CLARIFYING OUR RELIGIOUS identity is among the most important tasks facing religious liberals today. We cannot sustain effective prophetic practice unless we know who we are—unless we have a clear sense of our religious identity and a clear understanding of why prophetic social justice work is *religious* work. We must be clear about the core religious commitments and theological principles that support and guide this work.

Identity has never been easy for religious liberals. Our commitment to religious freedom, our openness to new ideas, our insistence that religion should live in the present and not in the past, our healthy theological pluralism—all of these, the very things that make us *liberal,* mean that our collective religious identity will inevitably be difficult to pin down at any particular moment. Lewis Fisher, dean of one of the early Universalist theological schools, captured this reality nearly a century ago as he considered the question of where Universalists stand. "The only true answer," he famously said, "is that we do not stand at all; we move."[209] The same could have been said for other religious liberals of his day and remains true today.

Historically, our most important struggles with identity have occurred when external circumstances or internal changes have forced us to reexamine our theologies. In the United States, perhaps the most important period in the shaping of our liberal theological identity was the nineteenth century, when first Universalists and Unitarians and then other Protestants began to develop theological stances in opposition to the dominant Calvinism and biblicism. They found God to be close and loving rather than distant and judgmental. They rejected the doctrine of election, which held that only a select few would be saved, claiming instead that all are saved. They believed human beings were basically good rather than tainted by original sin, and many challenged doctrinal claims about Jesus' divinity. Despite internal disagreements on some points, they achieved a theological clarity remarkable for liberals—a clarity we have not had since.

Other identity crises have emerged since that time. In the early twentieth century, the emergence of religious humanism pushed many religious liberals, principally Unitarians, in a distinctly post-Christian direction. Around the same time, other liberals were moving away from Christianity in a different direction, one that sought to expand the liberal principle of inclusiveness into a broad-based world religion. These moves created tensions with those who preferred to evolve within the liberal Christian framework, and the identity issues they raised lingered throughout the first half of the twentieth century. The string of mid-century liberal Protestant mergers that formed the United Church of Christ in 1957, the Unitarian Universalist Association in 1961, and the United Methodist Church in 1968, generated their own sets of identity tensions, although they were more often about institutional structures than theology.

Today, new religious identity issues arise as people struggle to define or redefine their faith commitments in light of the economic, political, ecological, and other uncertainties in which we live. While many find comfort in the certainties of dogmatic or fundamentalist faith, this option is off the table for religious liberals.

But if we don't have the certainty of dogma, what do we have? Do religious liberals share a set of core religious values or commitments that cut across credal and non-credal faith traditions and individual preferences? Or are we simply a loose collection of liberal spiritual seekers whose main commonality is the searching itself? We know we are theologically diverse; ironically, valuing diversity is one of the things we hold in common. But can we also point to deeper theological principles that identify us as religious liberals and hold us together as a larger faith tradition? How we answer these questions will affect both the course and the quality of liberal prophetic practice for the foreseeable future.

I believe that we do share a set of religious values and theological principles underlying our diverse individual and denominational orientations. One of our important tasks is to discover just what these core principles are—to name them and, if necessary, re-name them for our time. Despite our many differences, there is a reason we can all call ourselves religious liberals and have some basic understanding of what that means.

Below, I sketch a tentative understanding of the core theological principles that most religious liberals affirm. There is no unanimity here; indeed, unanimity among liberals is impossible to imagine. As I have continued to reflect on these ideas over the past few years, I have found that my own list and my ways of articulating it keep changing, so I invite argument and disagreement with what I think of as merely a conversation starter. These principles identify the common theological ground shared by religious liberals of all stripes, credal and non-credal, Christian, Jewish, Muslim, and more. Stated in abbreviated form, they require further development, a task I leave for future work.[210]

The fundamental unity and interdependence of all existence. Reality is relational, continuously recreated in a dynamic, open-ended evolutionary process that includes both social and ecological relationships. Human beings and the natural world constitute a single organic community in which the health, security, and well-being of each are intertwined with and dependent on the health, security, and well-being of all. There is no separation between *us* and *them*; we are all *us*.

The transforming power of love. We affirm the reality of love as a dynamic relational power within and among us. This power moves us to create relationships of compassion, respect, mutuality, and forgiveness; to love our neighbors as ourselves; and to recognize everyone as our neighbor.

The inherent worth and dignity of all persons. All human beings have the right to a meaningful and fulfilling life, including physical safety and economic and social well-being. All persons have an obligation to help create the conditions within which this well-being can be most fully realized.

Human freedom. Within the constraints of biological, historical, and cultural circumstances, human beings are free moral agents who make choices for which they are accountable. This freedom is expressed in our human striving for meaningful and fulfilling lives and for liberation from all forms of oppression. Human freedom may be used creatively or destructively. These possibilities are expressed not only in our individual choices and actions but also in the institutions and social structures we create.

Rejection of moral dualism. We reject as false the sharp separation of good and evil, refusing to assign individuals and nations into one category or the other. Moral dualism can blind us to our own capacity for evil and to the inherent worth and dignity of those whom we are tempted to see as *other*. Recognizing this moral ambiguity encourages us to cultivate the goodness in ourselves and others.

Social justice. Justice concerns the fair ordering of human relationships, including social, political, and ecological relationships. Just communities reflect equal concern for all, respect for basic human rights and liberties, non-coercive institutions, consensual relationships, shared power, and inclusiveness. Human beings have an obligation to create institutions, social structures, and environmental conditions that reflect these values and enable all persons to live with dignity and respect.

Cooperative power. Power is created and expressed in complex networks of human relationships. Power can be used to create or destroy, to liberate or oppress. Social justice and human fulfillment require the use of cooperative power—power with, not power over. Cooperative power is grounded in a commitment to mutual persuasion over coercion.

Religious freedom. We affirm the principles of freedom of conscience and religious free exercise, the separation of church and state, freedom of association, and freedom of dissent. All persons have an obligation to help create social and political structures within which these freedoms may be most fully realized.

Theological openness. Religious truth is not given just once for all time; we are therefore skeptical of all claims of finality, including our own. No belief system or historical moment has any unique status. Religious meaning is constructed rather than given and may come through many sources. We affirm the principle of free religious inquiry and the theological diversity that is the natural result of free inquiry.

With these principles in mind, let us consider an insight from Universalist heritage, an important but often overlooked part of our liberal religious tradition. If I were to give it a name and include it among the principles above, I might call it *human liberation.* But it is a form of liberation not grounded in any external source or individual merit or growth process. Instead, it is a liberation rooted in a commitment to radical human equality. This insight was originally articulated in the language of doctrines that are no longer part of the religious vocabulary of most liberals, but its theological implications remain powerful and relevant for us today.

Put simply, Universalism's core theological insight was that all humanity, indeed all of creation, is ultimately united in a common destiny. In contrast to the Calvinist doctrine of election, in which only a few of us—the elect—would be saved, Universalists held that all would be saved. Universalists refused to divide the world into factions or to exclude anyone from their vision. Instead, their theology was radically inclusive. It said that we're all in this together, and wherever we are headed, we will all share in it. The conviction that God would redeem all human souls became what historian Ann Lee Bressler calls "the integrating force" of the Universalist movement.[211]

This theology made Universalism a radically egalitarian communal faith. Here, the term *communal* refers to more than a group of individuals who share a common belief and come together for mutual support and worship, as we understand it today. In this inclusive communal theology, the individual was completely removed from the religious equation. Universalism insisted that individual merit had no bearing on salvation. In other words, one person's salvation is no more important than anyone else's. This theological stance challenged both the evangelical emphasis on individual conversion as the basis for salvation and the liberal emphasis on personal spiritual development and salvation as a process leading toward human fulfillment and perfectibility. Universalism taught that one's own personal welfare was inseparably linked to the welfare of all of humanity.

Moreover, because all human souls were deemed worthy of salvation regardless of individual merit, Universalism's understanding of egalitarianism was different from others. The American emphasis had always been on equality of opportunity, at least in principle, while in practice tolerating vast inequalities of outcome. Most Protestant denominations, both orthodox and liberal, shared what we might call this fair process-oriented understanding of equality. But Universalism's social doctrine, grounded in its radical theological doctrine, was "an egalitarianism not of opportunity, but of desert,"[212] or outcome. In other words, the principle of universal salvation generated a sense of wholeness and harmony that was the theological basis for a truly egalitarian society. Bressler summarizes:

> Universalism was a movement different in kind, not merely in degree, from the . . . other dissenting groups that "democratized" American Christianity in the early nineteenth century. Universalism effectively set aside the traditional psychological foci of religious belief—sin, guilt, repentance, and judgment—that absorbed and channeled human anxiety. . . . Universalism was

not for the faint-hearted, for it dismantled the common mental structures of faith and the security found therein.[213]

There is something theologically vital in the original Universalist insight that is worth preserving. If we restate this Universalist principle in the language of our own time, we might say that it is basically a commitment to human liberation, which has always been a central theme in religious liberalism. Unitarian Universalist theologian James Luther Adams noted a half century ago that liberalism's most characteristic feature is

> the conviction that human beings should be liberated, indeed should liberate themselves, from the shackles that impede religious, political, and economic freedom and which impede the appearance of a rational and voluntary piety and of equality and justice for all. . . . Liberalism's general idea has been to promote liberation from tyranny, provincialism, and arbitrariness, and thus to contribute to the meaningful fulfillment of human existence.[214]

Liberal Presbyterian theologian Peter Hodgson argues that if it is to fulfill its commitment to human freedom, "liberal theology must also be a liberation theology," a "*prophetic, culturally transformative* theology"[215] oriented toward social justice and overcoming oppression. He echoes Adams's emphasis on liberation in what he calls liberal theology's "freedom project."

> The freedom project entails above all the emancipation of human beings and human culture from oppressions stemming from colonialism, racism, classism, gender discrimination, homophobia, xenophobia, nationalism, consumerism, violence, economic and political injustice, ecological exploitation; the list goes on.[216]

Early Universalists understood, as do contemporary religious liberals, that liberation is social, that human fulfillment and liberation are possible only in a context of open and inclusive communities based on respect and justice. They recognized that spiritual liberation and social liberation are inextricably linked. Our contemporary theological commitments echo our early Universalist forebears' call for social justice built around a vision of a radically egalitarian society. Their call challenges us to pick up this mantle and carry on their quest, to reaffirm the deep commitment to human liberation that lies at the heart of liberal religion and fuels our prophetic practice.

In the end, of course, religious identity involves more than theology. Many factors contribute to our identity as religious liberals, including our music and worship practices, our racial and ethnic makeup, our educational and class profile, our politics, and what we might call our basic culture or even our religious style. But theological clarity is critical. Theological clarity affects more than self-understanding. It also affects the prophetic message we bring to the world. We know the challenges we face— a world awash in militarism and violence, a debilitating global economic crisis, dehumanizing poverty and suffering on all continents, life-threatening environmental disasters, persistent xenophobia and racism, and many more. Yet we also know there is a better way. As religious liberals, we know that we are united in a single interdependent world, that human beings have the ability to create good as well as evil, that our diversity is something to celebrate rather than fear, and that we can build just and liberating human communities. This is the message of healing and hope our prophetic social justice practice brings to the world.

Notes

1 See www.youtube.com/watch?feature=player_embedded&v= oPAJNntoRgA#!, accessed December 10, 2011. Also quoted in Jonathan Capehart, "Rick Perry ads draw blood," *Washington Post* blog posted December 9, 2011, www.washingtonpost.com/blogs/post-partisan/post/ rick-perry-ads-draw-blood/2011/03/04/gIQAClM7hO_blog.html, accessed December 10, 2011.

2 Todd Starnes, "Obama Leaves God out of Thanksgiving Address," http:// radio.foxnews.com/toddstarnes/top-stories/obama-leaves-god-out-of-thanksgiving-address.html, accessed December 10, 2011. See the presidential proclamation at www.whitehouse.gov/the-press-office/2011/11/16/ presidential-proclamation-thanksgiving-day-2011, accessed December 10, 2011.

3 See ABC news report, "Obama Leaves God out of Thanksgiving Speech, Riles Critics," at http://abcnews.go.com/Politics/obama-omits-god-thanksgiving-address-riles-critics/story?id=15028644#.TuOFqPKD9Wk, accessed December 10, 2011.

4 See the News Hounds website, www.newshounds.us/2011/07/28/is_fox_news_antimormon.php, accessed December 10, 2011.

5 The many works commenting on this development include Charles F. Andrain, *Political Justice and Religious Values* (New York: Routledge, 2008), esp. pages 134–157; Kevin Phillips, *American Theocracy: The Peril and Politics of Radical Religion, Oil, and Borrowed Money in the 21st Century* (New York: Viking, 2006); Michelle Goldberg, *Kingdom Coming: The Rise of Christian Nationalism* (New York: W.W. Norton, 2006); Mark Lewis Taylor, *Religion, Politics, and the Christian Right: Post-9/11 Powers and American Empire* (Minneapolis: Augsburg Fortress, 2005); and Rebecca T. Alpert, ed., *Voices of the Religious Left: A Contemporary Sourcebook* (Philadelphia: Temple University Press, 2000). See also Steven Kepnes, "Whither

Religious Liberals? Lamenting the Loss of Prophetic Voices, Weakened Chaplaincy," *Vital Theology*, 5, no. 1 (February 2008).

6 See Religion and Politics Survey, 2000, Princeton University, available on the American Religious Data Archive, at www.thearda.com/Archive/Files/Codebooks/RELPOL2000_CB.asp#V4, accessed November 27, 2011 (cited as Princeton Survey); John C. Green, *The American Religious Landscape and Political Attitudes: A Baseline for 2004* (Akron, OH: Ray C. Bliss Institute of Applied Politics, 2004), www.uakron.edu/bliss/research/archives/2004/Religious_Landscape_2004.pdf, accessed November 27, 2011 (cited as Bliss 2004 Study); and The Pew Forum on Religion and Public Life, *Many Americans Uneasy with Mix of Religion and Politics* (2006), at http://pewforum.org/docs/?DocID=153#about, accessed November 27, 2011.

7 Bliss 2004 Study, 12–14. The 15 percent figure is for modernist mainline Protestants. See also David Heim, "Voters and Values," *Christian Century* (August 8, 2006): 26–27.

8 Media Matters for America, *Left Behind: The Skewed Representation of Religion in Major News Media* (May 2007), http://mediamatters.org/reports/leftbehind/, accessed November 27, 2011. See also Media Matters for America, *If It's Sunday, It's Still Conservative: Special Report: How the Right Continues to Dominate the Sunday Talk Shows* (March 2007), http://cloudfront.mediamatters.org/static/pdf/if-its-sunday-its-still-conservative.pdf, accessed November 27, 2011.

9 E. J. Dionne Jr., *Souled Out: Reclaiming Faith and Politics After the Religious Right* (Princeton, NJ: Princeton University Press, 2008), 25.

10 Laura R. Olson, "Whither the Religious Left? Religiopolitical Progressivism in Twenty-First-Century America," in J. Matthew Wilson, ed., *From Pews to Polling Places: Faith and Politics in the American Religious Mosaic* (Washington, DC: Georgetown University Press, 2007), 53–79, 72.

11 Ibid., 57, 77.

12 Robert Wuthnow and John H. Evans, eds., *The Quiet Hand of God: Faith-Based Activism and the Public Role of Mainline Protestantism* (Berkeley: University of California Press, 2002), 401.

13 John C. Green, Robert P. Jones, and Daniel Cox, *Faithful, Engaged, and Divergent: A Comparative Portrait of Conservative and Progressive Religious Activists in the 2008 Election and Beyond* (Akron, OH: Ray C. Bliss

Institute of Applied Politics, 2009), 5, available at www.uakron.edu/bliss/
research/archives/2008/ReligiousActivistReport-Final.pdf, accessed
November 27, 2011.

[14] John C. Green, "A Liberal Dynamo: The Political Activism of the
Unitarian-Universalist Clergy," *Journal for the Scientific Study of Religion*,
42, no. 4 (2003): 577–590, 577, 589.

[15] See www.standingonthesideoflove.org/, accessed November 27, 2011. For
information on the Knoxville shooting incident, see Donald E. Skinner,
"Two Unitarian Universalists killed in church shooting," *UUWorld*, July 28,
2008, www.uuworld.org/news/articles/117286.shtml, accessed November
27, 2011.

[16] See "UUA President Sentenced to Time Served for Protest," in *UUWorld*,
August 29, 2011, www.uuworld.org/news/articles/186959.shtml, accessed
November 27, 2011.

[17] See www.standingonthesideoflove.org/blog/a-toolkit-how-you-can-help-
stop-deportations/, accessed December 10, 2011.

[18] See Shaila Dewan, "United Church of Christ Backs Same-Sex Marriage,"
New York Times, July 7, 2005, at www.nytimes.com/2005/07/05/national/
05church.html, accessed December 10, 2011. See the UCC Resolution at
www.ucc.org/assets/pdfs/2005-equal-marriage-rights-for-all-1.pdf, accessed
December 10, 2011.

[19] See www.ucc.org/god-is-still-speaking/about/, accessed December 10, 2011.

[20] Andrain, *Political Justice and Religious Values*, 25.

[21] Alan Wolfe, *The Future of Liberalism* (New York: Vintage Books, 2010), 80.

[22] For a more complete discussion of the characteristics of religious liberal-
ism, see Paul Rasor, *Faith Without Certainty: Liberal Theology in the 21st
Century* (Boston: Skinner House, 2005), 1–31, from which this discussion is
adapted. See also Gary Dorrien, *The Making of American Liberal Theology
Vol. 1: Imagining Progressive Religion 1805–1900* (Louisville: Westminster
John Knox, 2001), xiii–xxiii.

[23] The leading example is Francis Ellingwood Abbot, *Scientific Theism* (Boston: Little, Brown & Co., 1885).

[24] Sallie McFague, *The Body of God: An Ecological Theology* (Minneapolis:
Fortress, 1993), 76.

[25] See, e.g., Gordon D. Kaufman, *In Face of Mystery: A Constructive Theology*
(Cambridge: Harvard University Press, 1993), 45–59.

26 James Luther Adams, "Why Liberal?" *Journal of Liberal Religion*, 1, no. 2 (Autumn 1939): 3–8, 5.

27 John C. Green, "The Fifth National Survey of Religion and Politics: A Baseline for the 2008 Presidential Election," (Akron, OH: Ray C. Bliss Institute of Applied Politics, 2008), 25, available at www.uakron.edu/bliss/ research/archives/2008/Blissreligionreport.pdf, accessed November 27, 2011 (cited as Bliss 2008 Report). See also Bliss 2004 Report, 4.

28 See Gary Dorrien, *The Making of American Liberal Theology Vol. 1: Imagining Progressive Religion 1805–1900* (Louisville: Westminster John Knox, 2001), xv–xxi.

29 Gary Dorrien, *The Making of American Liberal Theology Vol. 3: Crisis, Irony, and Postmodernity 1950–2005* (Louisville: Westminster John Knox, 2006), 395–450.

30 See Religion and Politics Survey, 2000, Princeton University, available on the American Religious Data Archive, www.thearda.com/Archive/Files/ Codebooks/RELPOL2000_CB.asp#V4, accessed December 10, 2011 (cited as Princeton Survey).

31 Central Conference of American Rabbis, at http://ccarnet.org/Articles/ index.cfm?id=39&pge_prg_id=4687&pge_id=1656, accessed December 10, 2011. See also Michael A. Meyer, *A Response to Modernity: A History of the Reform Movement* (Detroit: Wayne State University Press, 1995).

32 Pew Forum on Religion and Public Life, *Religious Landscape Survey* (2008), 5, http://pewforum.org/US-Religious-Landscape-Survey-Resources. aspx (cited as Pew Landscape Survey).

33 Pew Landscape Survey, 5. See also Neil Gillman, *Conservative Judaism: The New Century* (Springfield, NJ: Behrman House, 1993).

34 Liberal Judaism also includes the Reconstructionist movement, which emerged in the early twentieth century, and interprets Judaism as an "evolving religious civilization" rather than a system of belief. The number of Jews identifying with Reconstructionism remains small; it is not a category in most surveys. See Rebecca T. Alpert and Jacob J. Staub, *Exploring Judaism: A Reconstructionist Approach*, 2nd ed. (New York: Reconstructionist Press, 2000).

35 Princeton Survey 2000. See Laura R. Olson, "Whither the Religious Left? Religiopolitical Progressivism in Twenty-First-Century America," in J. Matthew Wilson, ed., *From Pews to Polling Places: Faith and Politics in*

the American Religious Mosaic (Washington, DC: Georgetown University Press, 2007), 53–79.

36 See Pew Research Center for the People and the Press, "Muslim Americans: No Signs of Growth in Alienation or Support for Extremism" (August 30, 2011), www.people-press.org/2011/08/30/muslim-americans-no-signs-of-growth-in-alienation-or-support-for-extremism/, accessed November 27, 2011; Pew Research Center for the People and the Press, "Muslim Americans: Middle Class and Mostly Mainstream" (2007), http://pewresearch.org/assets/pdf/muslim-americans.pdf, accessed November 27, 2011.

37 Diana L. Eck, *A New Religious America: How a "Christian" Country Has Become the World's Most Religiously Diverse Nation* (New York: HarperCollins, 2001). Canada's religious diversity slightly exceeds that of the United States. Canada has a far higher percentage of non-Christian faiths, including more than four times as many Muslims, though about the same percentage of non-religious persons. See Statistics Canada, *Projections of the Diversity of the Canadian Population* (2010), www.statcan.gc.ca/pub/91-551-x/91-551-x2010001-eng.pdf, accessed November 27, 2011.

38 James Madison, "General Defense of the Constitution," June 12, 1788, in Robert S. Alley, ed., *James Madison on Religious Liberty* (Buffalo: Prometheus, 1985), 71.

39 Denise Lardner Carmody and John Tully Carmody, *The Republic of Many Mansions: Foundations of American Religious Thought* (New York: Paragon, 1990), 52–55.

40 Eck, *A New Religious America*, 239–243. See also Paul Rasor and Richard E. Bond, eds., *From Jamestown to Jefferson: The Evolution of Religious Freedom in Virginia* (Charlottesville: University of Virginia Press, 2011).

41 See William R. Hutchison, *Religious Pluralism in America: The Contentious History of a Founding Ideal* (New Haven, CT: Yale University Press, 2003), 111–132; Walter H. Conser Jr. and Sumner B. Twiss, *Religious Diversity and American Religious History* (Athens: University of Georgia Press, 1997), 1–26; and Eric Michael Mazur, *The Americanization of Religious Minorities: Confronting the Constitutional Order* (Baltimore: John Hopkins University Press, 1999).

42 Barry A. Kosmin and Ariela Keysar, *American Religious Identification Survey (ARIS) 2008* (Hartford, CT: Trinity College, 2009), 3, available

at http://commons.trincoll.edu/aris/files/2011/08/ARIS_Report_2008.pdf, accessed November 27, 2011 (cited as ARIS 2008 Survey).

43 Pew Landscape Survey, 5. See also Jon Meacham, "The Decline and Fall of Christian America," *Newsweek*, April 13, 2009.

44 See, e.g., Frank Lambert, *Religion in American Politics: A Short History* (Princeton, NJ: Princeton University Press, 2008), 218–250; Alpert, *Voices of the Religious Left*; Heim, "Voters and Values." For a helpful historical overview, see Daniel McKanan, "The Religious Left: An Old Tradition for a New Day," *UUWorld*, 23, no. 4 (Winter 2009): 27–32, available at http://www.uuworld.org/ideas/articles/151713.shtml, accessed November 27, 2011.

45 Steven H. Shiffrin, *The Religious Left and Church-State Relations* (Princeton, NJ: Princeton University Press, 2009), 1. As careful as Shiffrin is, he occasionally uses the terms inconsistently. On the very next page, he speaks of "religious liberalism" as "a form of liberalism that reaches liberal conclusions from religious premises." Ibid., 2; see also 106–107. But in general, his usage, and certainly his intention, is clear.

46 See the Sojourners mission statement at www.sojo.net/about-us/mission-statement, accessed February 19, 2012.

47 See the Tikkun statement at www.tikkun.org/nextgen/about, accessed February 19, 2012.

48 Green, et al., *Faithful, Engaged, and Divergent*, 1, 28. See also Lambert, *Religion in American Politics*, 222–223, and Robert P. Jones, *Progressive and Religious: How Christian, Jewish, Muslim, and Buddhist Leaders Are Moving Beyond the Culture Wars and Transforming American Public Life* (Lanham, MD: Rowman and Littlefield, 2008).

49 The Pew Landscape Survey and the ARIS 2008 are typical.

50 Bliss 2008 Survey, 26.

51 The 2008 Pew Religious Landscape Survey shows the total of all non-Christian faiths to be 4.7 percent of the U.S. population. If we assume that one-third are religiously liberal in the sense defined above—probably a conservative estimate—the total number of religious liberals would be approximately 21 percent.

52 Princeton Survey 2000. While this study is older than the others, the ARIS 2008 Survey notes that fewer changes took place in the first decade of this century than in the 1990s, suggesting that the Princeton findings should not differ much from what a similar study would show today.

[53] 24.8 percent of Protestants and other non-Catholics chose either fundamentalist or evangelical; 24.3 percent of Catholics chose traditionalist.

[54] The actual figure was 29.8 percent. For reasons that are not clear, comparable self-identity questions were apparently not asked of Jews and Muslims.
See Princeton Survey, questions 40 and 48.

[55] See Pew Landscaps Survey.

[56] James Luther Adams, "Why Liberal?" in *Journal of Liberal Religion*, 1
(Autumn 1939): 3–8, 6.

[57] Peter C. Hodgson, *Liberal Theology: A Radical Vision* (Minneapolis: Fortress, 2007), 21. Hodgson attributes this last statement to Edward Farley,
referring to Professor Farley's presentation to the American Academy of
Religion Consultation on Liberal Theologies in November 2005.

[58] See Norman K. Gottwald, *The Hebrew Bible: A Socio-Literary Introduction*
(Philadelphia: Fortress, 1985), 202–210. The social role of the biblical
prophets is discussed further in chapter five.

[59] Amos 8:4, NRSV.

[60] The U.S. Constitution, Art. VI, cl. 3, provides, "No religious test shall ever
be required as a qualification to any office or public trust under the United
States." The Supreme Court applied this rule to the states in *Torcaso v.
Watkins*, 367 U.S. 488 (1961). See Isaac Kramnick and R. Laurence Moore,
The Godless Constitution: A Moral Defense of the Secular State (New York:
W.W. Norton, 2005).

[61] Gottwald, *The Hebrew Bible*, 305.

[62] H. Richard Niebuhr, *Christ and Culture* (New York: Harper and Row,
1951), 84.

[63] Cornel West, *Prophetic Fragments: Illuminations of the Crisis in American
Religion and Culture* (Grand Rapids, MI: Wm. B. Eerdmans Publishing,
1988), ix.

[64] Gottwald, *The Hebrew Bible*, 307.

[65] Robert R. Wilson, *Prophecy and Society in Ancient Israel* (Philadelphia:
Fortress Press, 1980), 84.

[66] See Robert Wuthnow and John H. Evans, eds., *The Quiet Hand of God:
Faith-Based Activism and the Public Role of Mainline Protestantism* (Berkeley: University of California Press, 2002), 11–13; Laura R. Olson, "Whither
the Religious Left? Religiopolitical Progressivism in Twenty-First-Century
America," in J. Matthew Wilson, ed., *From Pews to Polling Places: Faith*

and Politics in the American Religious Mosaic (Washington, DC: George-town University Press, 2007), 63–64.

[67] See Robert Wuthnow, The Restructuring of American Religion (Princeton, NJ: Princeton University Press, 1988), 71–99. Cf. José Casanova, Public Religions in the Modern World (Chicago: University of Chicago Press, 1994), 52–55.

[68] H. Richard Niebuhr, The Social Sources of Denominationalism (New York: Holt, 1929), 82. Niebuhr is speaking here primarily of the churches within the Calvinist and Reformed denominations, but the same can be said of other liberal denominations. Many of today's more liberal groups, including the Unitarian Universalists and Congregationalists, emerged out of the Calvinist churches.

[69] Niebuhr, Christ and Culture, 104.

[70] Rebecca Chopp, The Praxis of Suffering: An Interpretation of Liberation and Political Theologies (Maryknoll, NY: Orbis, 1986), 122.

[71] Joerg Rieger, Remember the Poor: The Challenge to Theology in the Twenty-First Century (Harrisburg, PA: Trinity, 1998), 20.

[72] James Luther Adams, "The Changing Reputation of Human Nature" [1941], in George Kimmich Beach, ed., The Essential James Luther Adams: Selected Essays and Addresses (Boston: Skinner House, 1998), 59–60.

[73] See Sharon D. Welch, A Feminist Ethic of Risk (Minneapolis: Fortress, 1990), 14–15, 103–122.

[74] Ibid., 105.

[75] See Christopher Hinkle, "Pluralism's Problematic Appeal for Religious Liberals," paper delivered at the American Academy of Religion, November 2007, San Diego.

[76] See the sources cited in note 6.

[77] Hinkle, "Pluralism's Problematic Appeal," 2.

[78] See www.uua.org/statements/statements/13451.shtml, accessed December 11, 2011.

[79] An index of UUA resolutions on international peace and conflict can be found at www.uua.org/statements/results.php?ftst=regular&search_in_body=1&search_in_title=1&search_text=&topic=International%20Peace%20and%20Conflict&type=&from_year=&Submit=Submit, accessed December 11, 2011. In UUA practice, such statements may be called resolutions, actions or resolutions of immediate witness, or statements of conscience.

80 See www.uua.org/statements/statements/14422.shtml, accessed December 11, 2011.

81 See www.uua.org/statements/statements/185342.shtml, accessed December 11, 2011.

82 See www.uua.org/statements/statements/13394.shtml, accessed December 11, 2011. Full disclosure: I was a member of the advisory committee that drafted this statement and contributed some of its specific language.

83 David Robinson, *The Unitarians and the Universalists* (Westport, CT: Greenwood, 1985), 12.

84 The paradigmatic statement of this idea is in Friedrich Schleiermacher, *On Religion: Speeches to Its Cultural Despisers* [1799], trans. Richard Crouter (New York: Cambridge University Press, 1988). For a critique of the liberal emphasis on experience, see Paul Rasor, *Faith Without Certainty: Liberal Theology in the 21st Century* (Boston: Skinner House, 2005), 109–139.

85 See the Bylaws of the Unitarian Universalist Association, Section C-2.1., Principles, www.uua.org/uuagovernance/bylaws/articleii/6906.shtml, accessed November 1, 2011.

86 See Mark Chaves, *American Religion: Contemporary Trends* (Princeton, NJ: Princeton University Press, 2011), 61–62.

87 Recent studies of this phenomenon include Chris Hedges, *American Fascists: The Christian Right and the War on America* (New York: Free Press, 2006); Michelle Goldberg, *Kingdom Coming: The Rise of Christian Nationalism* (New York: W.W. Norton, 2006). See also George M. Marsden, *Understanding Fundamentalism and Evangelicalism* (Grand Rapids, MI: Wm. B. Eerdmans Publishing, 1991).

88 John Rawls, *Political Liberalism: Expanded Edition* (New York: Columbia University Press, 2005), xviii.

89 John Courtney Murray, *We Hold These Truths: Catholic Reflections on the American Proposition* (Kansas City, KS: Sheed & Ward, 1960), 15.

90 See "Introduction: The Pursuit of Religious Liberty in America," in Daniel L. Driesbach & Mark David Hall, eds., *The Sacred Rights of Conscience: Selected Readings on Religious Liberty and Church-State Relations in the American Founding* (Indianapolis: Liberty Fund, 2009); James H. Hutson, *Religion and the Founding of the American Republic* (Washington, DC: Library of Congress, 1998).

91 Examples include William Ellery Channing, "Importance of Religion to Society" [1830], in William Ellery Channing, *The Works of William Ellery Channing*, Vol. V (Boston: American Unitarian Association, 1903), 339–342; and ibid., Vol. IV, 67–103.

92 A useful collection of writings by the major figures on both sides can be found in J. Caleb Clanton, ed., *The Ethics of Citizenship: Liberal Democracy and Religious Convictions* (Waco, TX: Baylor University Press, 2009).

93 Jeffrey Stout, *Democracy and Tradition* (Princeton, NJ: Princeton University Press, 2004), 6.

94 Amy Gutmann and Dennis Thompson, *Why Deliberative Democracy?* (Princeton, NJ: Princeton University Press, 2004), 134.

95 Ibid., 4.

96 Kent Greenawalt, *Private Consciences and Public Reasons* (New York: Oxford University Press, 1995), 39.

97 Bruce Ackerman, *Social Justice in the Liberal State* (New Haven: Yale University Press, 1980), 10.

98 Bruce Ackerman, "Why Dialogue?" *Journal of Philosophy*, 86 (1989): 5–22, reprinted in Clanton, ed., *The Ethics of Citizenship*, 119–134, at 129–130 (emphasis original).

99 Richard Rorty, "Religion as a Conversation Stopper," *Common Knowledge*, 3 (1994): 1–6.

100 Steven Smith develops this argument in Steven D. Smith, *The Disenchantment of Secular Discourse* (Cambridge: Harvard University Press, 2010), 216–225.

101 Kent Greenawalt, *Religious Convictions and Political Choice* (New York: Oxford University Press, 1988), 231.

102 John Rawls, *Political Liberalism* (New York: Columbia University Press, 1993).

103 Ibid., 224–225.

104 Ibid., 214.

105 John Rawls, "The Idea of Public Reason Revisited," *University of Chicago Law Review*, 64 (1997): 756–807, reprinted in John Rawls, *Political Liberalism: Expanded Edition* (New York: Columbia University Press, 2005), 440–490, 462.

106 Ibid., 460.

[107] Examples include Robert Audi, *Religious Commitment and Secular Reason* (New York: Cambridge University Press, 2000), 34–35, 116–117; Brendan Sweetman, *Why Politics Needs Religion: The Place of Religious Arguments in the Public Square* (Downers Grove, IL: Intervarsity Press, 2006), 86–91; Bruce Ackerman, *Social Justice in the Liberal State* (New Haven: Yale University Press, 1980), 281.

[108] See Michael J. Perry, *Love and Power: The Role of Religion and Morality in American Politics* (New York: Oxford University Press, 1991), 25–26. The other book is Michael J. Perry, *Religion in Politics: Constitutional and Moral Perspectives* (New York: Oxford University Press, 1997).

[109] Michael J. Perry, *Under God? Religious Faith and Liberal Democracy* (Cambridge, UK: Cambridge University Press, 2003), 38–39.

[110] Ibid., 51.

[111] Christopher J. Eberle, *Religious Conviction in Liberal Politics* (Cambridge, UK: Cambridge University Press, 2002), 10.

[112] J. Caleb Clanton, "Democratic Deliberation *after* Religious Gag Rules," in Clanton, ed., *The Ethics of Citizenship*, 365–392, 368.

[113] Stout, *Democracy and Tradition*, 10.

[114] Smith, *The Disenchantment of Secular Discourse*, 39.

[115] Robin Lovin, "Perry, Naturalism, and Religion in Public," *Tulane Law Review*, 63 (1989): 1517–1539, 1531–1532.

[116] See "Opposition to the Illegal Immigration Reform and Immigrant Resolution Act," adopted in 2000, http://archives.umc.org/interior_print.asp?ptid=4&mid=1062, accessed December 28, 2011. The title of the resolution presumably refers to the Illegal Immigration Reform and Immigrant Responsibility Act, a federal law adopted in 1996.

[117] United Church of Christ Resolution of Witness Supporting International Human Rights Related to Sexual Orientation and Gender Identity, 2011, www.ucc.org/synod/resolutions/gs28/Resolution-on-Sexual-Orientation-Rights.pdf, accessed December 28, 2011.

[118] "Congressional Briefing by Rev. William G. Sinkford," July 11, 2006, in *Standing on the Side of Love, 2008: No Discrimination in Our Constitutions*, UUA Office of Congregations, Washington Office of Advocacy, 17–18, www.uua.org/documents/washingtonoffice/08_marriage_equality.pdf, accessed December 27, 2011. See also http://archive.uua.org/president/060711_ftm.html, accessed November 14, 2011.

[119] The U.S. Supreme Court ruled that these so-called anti-miscegenation laws were unconstitutional in the landmark case of *Loving v. Virginia*, 388 U.S. 1 (1967).

[120] See http://archive.uua.org/president/060711_ftm.html, accessed December 27, 2011.

[121] Hearings before the Subcommittee on Courts, Civil Liberties, and the Administration of Justice of the Committee on the Judiciary, House of Representatives, 96th Congress, 2nd Sess., on S. 540, July 29–30, August 19, 21, and September 9, 1980. This bill did not become law.

[122] The leading case is *Engle v. Vitale*, 370 U.S. 421 (1962).

[123] 374 U.S. 203 (1963).

[124] Hearings, 149, 152, 154. In 2011, the U.S. branch of Campus Crusade for Christ officially changed its name to Cru. See www.ccci.org/about-us/donor-relations/our-new-name/press.htm, accessed November 14, 2011. William Bright died in 2003; see http://billbright.ccci.org/public/, accessed on November 14, 2011.

[125] Hearings, 292–294.

[126] The June 2011 report of the First Amendment Center indicates that two-thirds (67 percent) of Americans agree that the First Amendment requires a clear separation of church and state, while 28 percent disagree. See "State of the First Amendment 2011," www.firstamendmentcenter.org/madison/wp-content/uploads/2011/07/sofa-2011-report.pdf, accessed November 19, 2011.

[127] Laura R. Olson, "Whither the Religious Left? Religiopolitical Progressivism in Twenty-First-Century America," in J. Matthew Wilson, ed., *From Pews to Polling Places: Faith and Politics in the American Religious Mosaic* (Washington, DC: Georgetown University Press, 2007), 53–79, 78.

[128] Derek H. Davis, "From Engagement to Retrenchment: An Examination of First Amendment Activism by America's Mainline Churches, 1980–2000," in Robert Wuthnow and John H. Evans, eds., *The Quiet Hand of God: Faith-Based Activism and the Public Role of Mainline Protestantism* (Berkeley: University of California Press, 2002), 321–324.

[129] See Erwin Chemerinsky, *Constitutional Law: Principles and Policies*, 4th ed. (New York: Wolters Kluwer, 2011), 1236–1243, 1297–1306.

[130] Davis, "From Engagement to Retrenchment," 318.

131 James E. Wood Jr., "Public Religion vis a vis the Prophetic Role of Religion," *Journal of Church and State*, 41 (1999): 51–76, 53.

132 *Walz v. Tax Commission of the City of New York*, 397 U.S. 644, 670 (1970). The case involved a challenge to a state law granting tax exemptions for property used for religious, educational, or charitable purposes; the Court upheld the law.

133 *McDaniel v. Paty*, 435 U.S. 618, 640–41 (1978).

134 Deut. 18:18, NRSV.

135 See Robert R. Wilson, *Prophecy and Society in Ancient Israel* (Philadelphia: Fortress Press, 1980), 28–32; Walter Houston, *Contending for Justice: Ideologies and Theologies of Social Justice in the Old Testament* (London: T&T Clark, 2006), 93–98.

136 This view is especially associated with Max Weber. See Max Weber, *The Sociology of Religion* [1922], trans. Talcott Parsons (Boston: Beacon Press, 1993), 46–59 and passim.

137 See Norman K. Gottwald, *The Hebrew Bible: A Socio-Literary Introduction* (Philadelphia: Fortress, 1985), 307.

138 Ibid.; Wilson, *Prophecy and Society*, 28, 40.

139 Robert Wilson makes this point about Jeremiah and suggests that it may have been true of Isaiah of Jerusalem as well. See Wilson, *Prophecy and Society*, 241–242, 272–273.

140 See Wilson, *Prophecy and Society*, 71.

141 Ibid., 84.

142 D. N. Premnath, *Eighth Century Prophets: A Social Analysis* (St. Louis: Chalice Press, 2003), 43–98.

143 Isa. 1:23; see also 10:1–4.

144 Amos 2:6, 8. On pledges taken as security for loans, see Exod. 22:26 and Deut. 24:12–13.

145 Premnath, *Eighth Century Prophets*, 182.

146 On the nature of covenant, see Gottwald, *The Hebrew Bible*, 202–207. For a discussion of the humanitarian nature of biblical laws relating to lending, see Paul B. Rasor, "Biblical Roots of Modern Consumer Credit Law," *Journal of Law and Religion*, 10 (1993): 157–192, at 164–167.

147 Deut. 16:18–17:20. See also Wilson, *Prophecy and Society*, 160.

148 Deut. 18:9–22.

149 Abraham J. Heschel, *The Prophets*, vol. II (New York: Harper and Row, 1962), 258–260.

150 1 Sam 13:5–15; see Wilson, *Prophecy and Society*, 181.

151 2 Sam. 11:1–27.

152 James Luther Adams, "The Prophetic Covenant and Social Concern" [1977], in James Luther Adams, *An Examined Faith: Social Context and Religious Commitment*, George K. Beach, ed. (Boston: Beacon Press, 1991), 234–242, 240–241. See also James Luther Adams, "Mediating Structures and the Separation of Powers" [1980], in J. Ronald Engel, ed., *Voluntary Associations: Socio-cultural Analyses and Theological Interpretation* (Chicago: Exploration, 1986), 217–249.

153 See, e.g., *New York Times v. Sullivan*, 376 U.S. 254 (1964).

154 Cornel West, *Democracy Matters: Winning the Fight Against Imperialism* (New York: Penguin Books, 2004), 14.

155 See Sheldon S. Wolin, *Politics and Vision Continuity and Innovation in Western Political Thought*, expanded ed. (Princeton, NJ: Princeton University Press, 2004), 559–562; Andrew J. Bacevich, *Washington Rules: America's Path to Permanent War* (New York: Metropolitan Books, 2010), 8–18, 182–221.

156 Andrew J. Bacevich, *The Limits of Power: The End of American Exceptionalism* (New York: Metropolitan Books, 2008), 68.

157 Bacevich, *Washington Rules*, 250.

158 West, *Democracy Matters*, 2.

159 Sheldon S. Wolin, *Democracy Incorporated: Managed Democracy and the Specter of Inverted Totalitarianism* (Princeton, NJ: Princeton University Press, 2008), 132.

160 Bacevich, *Washington Rules*, 14 and passim.

161 Wolin, *Democracy Incorporated*, xvii and passim.

162 West, *Democracy Matters*, 3. West also names a third such dogma "escalating authoritarianism," but I consider it a general trend that includes the other two.

163 Andrew J. Bacevich, *The New American Militarism: How Americans Are Seduced by War* (New York: Oxford University Press, 2005).

164 Bacevich, *Washington Rules*, 210.

165 President Obama's Remarks at the National Defense University, March 12, 2009, www.ndu.edu/chds/docUploaded/President%20Obama%20Speech%20NDU.pdf, accessed December 13, 2011.

[166] See Bacevich, *Washington Rules*, 25; Jack Nelson-Pallmeyer, *Saving Christianity from Empire* (New York: Continuum, 2005), 97–98.

[167] Nelson-Pallmeyer, *Saving Christianity*, 97.

[168] Bacevich, *New Militarism*, 33, quoting C. Wright Mills.

[169] Walter Wink, *Engaging the Powers: Discernment and Resistance in a World of Domination* (Minneapolis: Fortress Press, 1992), 13–31.

[170] Wink, *Engaging the Powers*, 13.

[171] Stanley Hauerwas, "Sacrificing the Sacrifices of War," in Stanley Hauerwas, *War and the American Difference: Theological Reflections on Violence and National Identity* (Grand Rapids, MI: Baker Academic, 2011), 53–70, 54.

[172] Bacevich, *New Militarism*, 1.

[173] Harvey Cox, "The Market as God," *The Atlantic Monthly* (March 1999), reprinted in Philip Zaleski, ed., *The Best Spiritual Writing 2000* (New York: HarperCollins, 2000), 70–82, 72.

[174] See Nomi Prins, *It Takes a Pillage: An Epic Tale of Power, Deceit, and Untold Trillions* (New York: Wiley, 2010); Matt Taibbi, *Griftopia: A Story of Bankers, Politicians, and the Most Audacious Power Grab in American History* (New York: Spiegel and Grau, 2011).

[175] Gordon Bigelow, "Let There Be Markets: The Evangelical Roots of Economics," *Harpers* (May 2005): 33–38, available at http://harpers.org/archive/2005/05/0080538, accessed December 13, 2011.

[176] See Richard J. Meagher, "Tax Revolt as a Family Value: How the Christian Right Is Becoming a Free Market Champion," *The Public Eye Magazine* (Winter 2006), www.publiceye.org/magazine/v21n1/meagher_tax_revolt.html, accessed December 13, 2011. See also the Internal Revenue Service discussion of the estate tax at www.irs.gov/businesses/small/article/0,,id=164871,00.html, accessed December 13, 2011.

[177] Bigelow, "Let There Be Markets."

[178] Hans Achterhuis, *De utopia van de vrije markt* [The Utopia of the Free Market] (Rotterdam: Lemniscaat, 2010).

[179] Wolin, *Democracy Incorporated*, xxi.

[180] Ibid., 34.

[181] Ibid., 237.

[182] Bacevich, *Washington Rules*, 246.

[183] Wolin, *Democracy Incorporated*, 239.

[184] Wolin, *Politics and Vision*, 578.

[185] See Steven D. Smith, *The Disenchantment of Secular Discourse* (Cambridge: Harvard University Press, 2010), 6–18.

[186] Wolin, *Democracy Incorporated*, 59–60.

[187] Wendy R. Weiser and Lawrence Norden, *Voting Law Changes in 2012* (New York: Brennan Center for Justice, 2011), available at www.brennancenter.org/content/resource/voting_law_changes_in_2012/, accessed December 14, 2011. See also Michael Cooper, "New State Rules Raising Hurdles at Voting Booth," *New York Times*, October 2, 2011, available at www.nytimes.com/2011/10/03/us/new-state-laws-are-limiting-access-for-voters.html?_r=1, accessed December 14, 2011.

[188] See Charlie Savage, "Holder Signals Tough Review of New State Laws on Voting," *New York Times*, December 13, 2011, available at www.nytimes.com/2011/12/14/us/politics/in-speech-holder-to-critique-new-voting-laws.html?pagewanted=1&_r=1&nl=todaysheadlines&emc=tha23, accessed December 14, 2011.

[189] West, *Democracy Matters*, 60.

[190] Wolin, *Democracy Incorporated*, 259.

[191] Bacevich, *Washington Rules*, 244–247.

[192] Wolin, *Democracy Incorporated*, 238.

[193] A more extended discussion of these commonalities and differences can be found in Paul Rasor, "Theological and Political Liberalisms," *Journal of Law and Religion*, 24 (2009): 433–462.

[194] See Peter C. Hodgson, *Liberal Theology: A Radical Vision* (Minneapolis: Fortress Press, 2007), 20; Gordon D. Kaufman, *In Face of Mystery: A Constructive Theology* (Cambridge: Harvard University Press, 1993), 42.

[195] Michael J. Perry, *Under God? Religious Faith and Liberal Democracy* (New York: Cambridge University Press, 2003), 36 (emphasis original).

[196] Wolin, *Democracy Incorporated*, 260.

[197] Ronald Dworkin, *A Matter of Principle* (Cambridge: Harvard University Press, 1985), 183.

[198] Ronald Dworkin, *Sovereign Virtue: The Theory and Practice of Equality* (Cambridge: Harvard University Press, 2000), 1.

[199] Wolin, *Democracy Incorporated*, 260–261.

[200] West, *Democracy Matters*, 16.

[201] Sharon D. Welch, *A Feminist Ethic of Risk* (Minneapolis: Fortress Press, 1990), 106.

202 West, *Democracy Matters*, 17.

203 Ibid., 16.

204 See Welch, *A Feminist Ethic of Risk*, 103–122.

205 Ibid., 75.

206 Ibid., 20.

207 West, *Democracy Matters*, 217.

208 Stout, *Democracy and Tradition*, 58–60.

209 Quoted in Charles A. Howe, *The Larger Faith: A Short History of American Universalism* (Boston: Skinner House, 1993), 96.

210 For another way of naming liberal religious principles relating to social justice, see Rebecca Parker, "Our Work for Social Justice," in Peter Morales, ed., *The Unitarian Universalist Pocket Guide*, 5th ed. (Boston: Skinner House, 2012).

211 Ann Lee Bressler, *The Universalist Movement in America, 1770–1880* (New York: Oxford University Press, 2001), 34.

212 Ibid., 37.

213 Ibid., 41–42.

214 James Luther Adams, "The Liberal Christian Looks at Himself" [1956], reprinted as "The Liberal Christian Holds Up the Mirror," in James Luther Adams, *An Examined Faith: Social Context and Religious Commitment*, George K. Beach, ed. (Boston: Beacon Press, 1991), 308–322, 311–312.

215 Peter C. Hodgson, *Liberal Theology: A Radical Vision* (Minneapolis: Fortress Press, 2007), 20, 19 (emphasis original).

216 Ibid., 69. Hodgson develops this liberal "freedom project" at length, 67–98.

For Further Reading

Andrain, Charles F. *Political Justice and Religious Values*. New York: Routledge, 2008.

Buehrens, John A., and Rebecca Ann Parker. *A House for Hope: The Promise of Progressive Religion for the Twenty-First Century*. Boston: Beacon Press, 2010.

Dionne, E. J., Jr. *Souled Out: Reclaiming Faith and Politics After the Religious Right*. Princeton, NJ: Princeton University Press, 2008.

Hodgson, Peter C. *Liberal Theology: A Radical Vision*. Minneapolis: Fortress, 2007.

McKanan, Dan. *Prophetic Encounters: Religion and the American Radical Tradition*. Boston: Beacon Press, 2011.

Millspaugh, John Gibb, ed. *A People So Bold: Theology and Ministry for Unitarian Universalists*. Boston: Skinner House, 2010.

Parker, Rebecca. *Blessing the World: What Can Save Us Now*. Robert Hardies, ed. Boston: Skinner House, 2006.

Rasor, Paul. *Faith Without Certainty: Liberal Theology in the 21st Century*. Boston: Skinner House, 2005.

Smith, Steven D. *The Disenchantment of Secular Discourse.* Cambridge: Harvard University Press, 2010.

Welch, Sharon. *A Feminist Ethic of Risk.* Revised Edition. Minneapolis: Fortress, 2000.

West, Cornel. *Democracy Matters: Winning the Fight Against Imperialism.* New York: Penguin, 2004.

Wolfe, Alan. *The Future of Liberalism.* New York: Vintage, 2010.

Wolin, Sheldon S. *Democracy Incorporated: Managed Democracy and the Specter of Inverted Totalitarianism.* Princeton, NJ: Princeton University Press, 2008.